The Effective School Governor

A Practical Guide to Assessing and Improving your Personal Effectiveness

David Marriott

Published by Network Educational Press Ltd.
PO Box 635
Stafford
ST16 1BF

First Published 1998
© David Marriott 1998

ISBN 1 85539 042 6

David Marriott asserts the moral right to be
identified as the author of this work

Series Editor - Tim Brighouse
Edited by Chris Griffin
Design & layout by
Neil Hawkins of Devine Design

Printed in Great Britain by
Redwood Books, Trowbridge, Wilts.

Acknowledgements

My understanding of the nature and needs of school governors stems from seven years spent working with governors as a Deputy Head, as a parent governor and as a governor trainer and developer. I would like to thank all the governors with whom I have worked and from whom I have learned an enormous amount. I would like to pay a particular tribute to the governors of schools in Wiltshire and Swindon, whose commitment to training and development is an example to all governors.

I would like to celebrate the work and enthusiasm of my colleagues in Governor Support in Wiltshire and Swindon, without whose unstinting efforts and creativity my work would have been impossible and my life the poorer.

Especial thanks go to Valerie Crute for her timely interventions in helping me to keep sight of my personal goals, especially at times of great uncertainty and insecurity.

Many thanks to Debbie, Duncan and Catherine for their tolerance of the time I spent writing this book instead of being with them.

David Marriott
February, 1998

Foreword

A teacher's task is much more ambitious than it used to be and demands a focus on the subtleties of teaching and learning and on the emerging knowledge of school improvement.

This is what this series is about.

Teaching can be a very lonely activity. The time honoured practice of a single teacher working alone in the classroom is still the norm; yet to operate alone is, in the end to become isolated and impoverished. This series addresses two issues – the need to focus on practical and useful ideas connected with teaching and learning and the wish thereby to provide some sort of an antidote to the loneliness of the long distance teacher who is daily berated by an anxious society.

Teachers flourish best when, in key stage teams or departments (or more rarely whole schools), their talk is predominantly about teaching and learning and where, unconnected with appraisal, they are privileged to observe each other teach; to plan and review their work together; and to practise the habit of learning from each other new teaching techniques. But how does this state of affairs arise? Is it to do with the way staffrooms are physically organised so that the walls bear testimony to interesting articles and in the corner there is a dedicated computer tuned to 'conferences' about SEN, school improvement, the teaching of English etc., and whether, in consequence, the teacher leaning over the shoulder of the enthusiastic IT colleagues sees the promise of interesting practice elsewhere? Has the primary school cracked it when it organises successive staff meetings in different classrooms and invites the 'host' teacher to start the meeting with a 15 minute exposition of their classroom organisation and management? Or is it the same staff sharing, on a rota basis, a slot on successive staff meeting agenda when each in turn reviews a new book they have used with their class? And what of the whole school which now uses 'active' and 'passive' concerts of carefully chosen music as part of their accelerated learning techniques?

It is of course well understood that excellent teachers feel threatened when first they are observed. Hence the epidemic of trauma associated with OFSTED. The constant observation of the teacher in training seems like that of the learner driver. Once you have passed your test and can drive unaccompanied, you do. You often make lots of mistakes and sometimes get into bad habits. Woe betide, however, the back seat driver who tells you so. In the same way the new teacher quickly loses the habit of observing others and being observed. So how do we get a confident, mutual observation debate going? One school I know found a simple and therefore brilliant solution. The Head of the History Department asked that a young colleague plan lessons for her – the Head of Department – to teach. This lesson she then taught, and was observed by the young colleague. There was subsequent discussion, in which the young teacher asked,

> *"Why did you divert the question and answer session I had planned?"*
> *and was answered by,*
> *"Because I could see that I needed to arrest the attention of the group by the window with some "hands-on" role play, etc."*

This lasted an hour and led to a once-a-term repeat discussion which, in the end, was adopted by the whole school. The whole school subsequently changed the pattern of its meetings to consolidate extended debate about teaching and learning. The two teachers claimed that because one planned and the other taught both were implicated but neither alone was responsible or felt 'got at'.

So there are practices which are both practical and more likely to make teaching a rewarding and successful activity. They can, as it were, increase the likelihood of a teacher surprising the pupils into understanding or doing something they did not think they could do rather than simply entertaining them or worse still occupying them. There are ways of helping teachers judge the best method of getting pupil expectation just ahead of self-esteem.

This series focuses on straightforward interventions which individual schools and teachers use to make life more rewarding for themselves and those they teach. Teachers deserve nothing less, for they are the architects of tomorrow's society, and society's ambition for what they achieve increases as each year passes.

Professor Tim Brighouse.

Contents

Tasks

Introduction

How can you become an Effective School Governor?

Whether you are thinking about becoming a governor, are a new governor or an experienced governor, this book will help you to become more effective by:

- *Encouraging you to reflect on your values, motivation and goals in life.*

- *Helping you to analyse the source of your personal authority and the skills, interests, abilities and personal qualities you can offer.*

- *Showing you how to apply these attributes to the role of school governor, recognising the limits to what a volunteer can achieve.*

- *Providing ways of identifying and meeting your development needs.*

- *Exploring how you can become an influential member of your governing body by understanding better how groups work.*

- *Examining ways of making an effective personal contribution to the work and development of the governing body.*

- *Encouraging a focus on the future in developing relationships and planning for continuity.*

Much emphasis has been placed, rightly, on the effectiveness of governing bodies as teams: rightly, because individual governors have power only as part of the collective body. Increasingly, Ofsted reports comment on the effectiveness of the governing body in the overall achievement of the school. Some excellent books are available to help governing bodies evaluate and develop themselves (for example, Michael Creese's **"Effective Governors, Effective Schools"**). Any governing body wishing to improve its collective practice can find much that will help them in the task.

However, each member of any governing body is an individual and is more or less effective in that role. Just as school improvement depends ultimately on the improvement of each student's performance, so the quality of individual governors is what contributes primarily to the effectiveness of the governing body as a whole.

The approach taken in this book is to focus on the development of the individual governor rather than the group, not because the group doesn't matter, but because every governing body is, first and foremost, a collection of individuals. It is likely that an individual governor will be more self-analytical and more willing to improve personal performance than the group. As each individual improves, so the group as a whole evolves into a more effective governing body.

The book is in three sections:

- *The first section requires you to think through what makes you tick as a person, rather than as a governor.*

Understanding your values, what motivates you and what goals you have, can help you to become more effective in various aspects of your life - including your role as a school governor. Being effective means using your authority. Understanding where your authority comes from can help you to use it more effectively. Analysing your interests, skills and abilities and personal qualities forms a useful basis for developing as a person and as a governor.

- *The second section helps you to answer the question: how can I be an effective governor? It looks closely at how you can apply what you have learned about yourself to the role.*

Governors' roles and responsibilities are numerous and varied. It is important that all governors understand what these are and how to fulfil them. Just as important, however, is to know how to play a more active and effective individual part in the practical workings of the governing body and its influence on the school.

Section Two, therefore, looks at your goals and motivation as a governor, and applies what you did in *Section One* to that role. It also explores the necessary limits to your commitment as a governor and how best to use your interests, skills and personal qualities in the work. *Section Two* concludes with an assessment of your training and development needs and an exploration of your induction.

- Following this exploration of how you can be an effective individual governor, *the third section looks at ways in which you can be effective as a team member of the governing body.*

New governors often join governing bodies that contain a real mixture of colleagues. Some of their fellow governors are...

H ighly

I mpressive

P rofessional

P eople with

O utstanding

S kills

...you might, however, meet a   **R** eally

H ere

I n

N ame

O nly

Whilst the governing body should, in an ideal world, work as an effective team, the harsh reality can sometimes be disappointingly different. Finding ways of being personally effective in a group of variously effective people is quite a challenge. You can improve the effectiveness of the whole group through setting an example, influencing decisions and developing good relationships with and between colleagues.

The question whether a governing body can become an effective team is dealt with here, as well as the roles people play in the group. I look at your role and suggest ways in which you might become more effective in meetings, including committees and full governing body meetings. I examine some of the wider aspects of the work beyond meetings, including visiting the school and the classroom, developing partnerships, and succession planning and continuity. This last point is very important. People do not stay for ever. Planning to ensure continuity and a smooth transition for when they leave is essential.

At the end of the book you will find an appendix of governors' roles and responsibilities, and a list of books and other resources which will be of interest to you and provide further support.

How to use the book

- As you work through each section, you will have the opportunity to try various tasks which will help you reflect on your experience and understanding and to ensure that you become more effective in your role.

- Try to work through the tasks systematically and in the sequence in which they occur, because each section builds on the tasks undertaken in the preceding sections.

- Keep your work on each task in a book or folder. You will need to refer to it.

- Constraints of time, or your personal interests, may mean you prefer to do the tasks on a more random basis. You will find it helpful to read the commentaries which precede the tasks in order to gain fuller benefit from each task.

- There is no need to undertake tasks if you are confident that you already know the answer(s).

- In many cases, sharing the task with a friend, colleague or acquaintance can be helpful. When appropriate, I draw attention to this in the text.

- It is a good idea to pace yourself. Don't try to do everything in a short space of time. Working through the book might take a week, a month or even a year or more: it is up to you to decide how fast you want to go.

- The book can act as a "First Aid Manual" to which you may refer when a particular issue or problem arises in your work as a governor.

Whichever approach you use, try to bear in mind that the book is about you; your development as a governor; and your contribution to the governing body and, subsequently, the work of the school. The more successfully you fulfil your role, the greater the chances of your school successfully educating its pupils. Good luck!

Personal Effectiveness

This book focuses on improving your effectiveness as an individual governor and as a member of a governing body. However, you are, first and foremost, an individual human being. Before asking "Why am I a governor and how can I do the job better?" it's a good idea to ask yourself "Who am I? What makes me tick? What do I want out of life?" Without some initial self-evaluation, your ability to analyse and improve your effectiveness as a governor will be limited and a little superficial.

Let's be clear, though: I'm not suggesting a course of psychoanalysis! Your self-reflection should involve, for example, consideration of the things you hold dear and value in others. School governors are volunteers, so my guess would be that you believe in public service, distrust materialism for its own sake and believe in a sense of community. Your other values will have developed through personal experience and you will be able to define these for yourself, with a little help. Without too much trouble, you'll also be able to list the things that interest you, your skills, abilities and personal qualities. Making these *implicit* personal matters *explicit* is an important first step, before you consider how you might apply and develop them in your role as a governor.

Let me put it another way. I could start by listing the roles and responsibilities of school governors and asking you to match yourself against them. It would be a pragmatic approach, but would risk limiting your potential development unnecessarily. You may well have all sorts of qualities, values and skills which could transform the role and find a variety of applications in the work. One of the rewards of learning to be an effective governor is personal development, so rather than wearing the role as a straitjacket, consider your potential and make the role fit you.

As you progress through this section, I will provide questions and challenges to encourage self-evaluation.

By the end of this section you will have listed and considered:

- ☛ *Your values*
- ☛ *What motivates you*
- ☛ *Your goals in life*
- ☛ *Where your authority comes from*
- ☛ *Your interests, skills and abilities and personal qualities*

What is an effective person?

Effective people get things done; live a full and satisfying life; know how to get the best out of any situation. They excel at everything. Don't they make you sick?

But, on the other hand, the pursuit of excellence seems to be self-evidently worthwhile. Who wants to settle for the second-rate? The recent White Paper, **"Excellence in Schools"** (The Stationery Office, 1997) advocated excellence for everyone. Who could object to such aims? Who could be against virtue? We all want the best for our children. We shouldn't tolerate failure.

Excellence, though, is a relative term, implying a hierarchy or continuum. It could be argued that "excellence for all" is a contradiction in terms, since an excellent school can only be defined in comparison to one which is not so good. Can there be degrees of excellence? I am not indulging in pedantry for its own sake because a culture of perfection can be very damaging and counter-productive. The excellent can drive out the good. Bruno Bettelheim, the psychoanalyst and survivor of Dachau and Buchenwald, promoted the idea of the *good enough* parent (**"A Good Enough Parent"**, Bettelheim, B., Vintage Books ,1987). He argued that, in striving to be the perfect mother or father, people develop feelings of guilt and inadequacy that prevent them from becoming *good enough* parents, which is all that really matters.

Good enough, the best possible in the circumstances, is good enough. We don't have to be perfect people to be successful and make a worthwhile contribution to our world and our society. So, when you consider your role as a governor, be realistic about what is possible, given the enormous range of responsibilities and the voluntary nature of the work. *Good enough is good enough.* Being effective is not the same thing as being perfect. Effectiveness brings satisfaction and makes difficult tasks possible.

You can judge your effectiveness as a person through self-reflection. It may help to ask a friend, colleague or partner to help you in this process, since another pair of eyes can provide a refreshing perspective. I want you to look at, and think about, your *values, what motivates* you, and *your goals in life.* Some people are more like leaders than others. Look at where their authority comes from and where you find yours. I will also help you to analyse your *interests, skills and abilities and personal qualities.*

1   Your Values

Task 1
Your Values

Draw or describe your ideal person. (You could base this on somebody you look up to.) Make a list of his or her characteristics that you admire.

Example *My ideal person is down-to-earth, has a good sense of humour and is always willing to listen. He/she will keep a secret and tell me when I'm wrong in a way that doesn't hurt my feelings. He/she is quiet but has strong opinions...*

Do the same for the sort of person you would hate to be, or somebody you dislike or disapprove of.

Example *I would hate to be the sort of person who judges everything by its monetary value. The kind of person who expects everyone else to obey but who never thanks you...*

Your drawing or description will reflect the values you hold dear. Everyone has his or her own values, whether he or she is conscious of them or not. Our values are fundamental to the decisions we take, the relationships and the choices we make. Sometimes when they are written down, they can seem bland or a wish-list. Words like trust, honesty and integrity are easy to say. Try comparing your list of values with the Nolan Committee's seven principles of public life (explained in greater detail on pages 48-49)

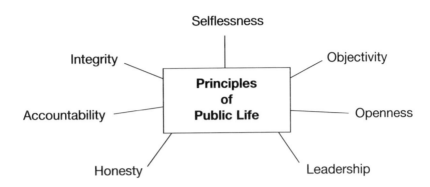

Your list might be very similar, suggesting that your personal values may have been developed through professional experience in the field of public service, though not necessarily. The Nolan Committee's principles are in many ways a reflection of the way in which most of us would like to see our MPs, local councillors and other public servants behaving. The public outcry - or at least the newspaper headlines - when a new story of political "sleaze" emerges, reminds us of how strongly we feel when our basic values are challenged. Our upbringing and education have reinforced such values as we have grown.

If your list is different, it is probably because you were not yet seeing your values in the context of public life, which is what I will ask you to do in *Section Two*. Whatever your response, the important point is that the apparent blandness of the words themselves should not distract us from the profound personal meaning they have for us. Like excellence, who could object to the words? They only become disembodied concepts when written down. We all *embody* personal values that have a huge effect on the way we live. When we recognise similar values in other people, we warm to them. When we feel obscurely offended by a decision that might appear to be entirely rational, it is often because it is at odds with one or more of our inherent values. It may well take us some time to work out why we feel offended because our values run so deep.

Education is far from being a value-free zone. In carrying out your roles and responsibilities as a governor, your values will be challenged. You will need to evaluate - make value judgements, in all sorts of ways.

For example, you will find that teachers do not teach in the same way as they did when you were at school. For example, you might be tempted, without thinking, to criticise the way children are grouped around tables, each working on different tasks from the others. Perhaps, when you were at school, the teacher taught from the front while you sat in a row of desks. You may honestly believe this to be a better approach. What's required is some discussion with the Head and staff about why they do things the way they do. You may or may not be convinced at the end, but I would hope that in the process you would have begun to question your own values, as well as those of the teachers in the school.

Being conscious of, and clear about, your values will help you to understand and work with your emotional responses to issues and decisions. However, the line between values and prejudices is a fine one. It is important to remain self-critical when your values are challenged. Checking out your reactions to such challenges with a good and trusted friend can help to clarify whether your reactions are positive and healthy or based on preconceived opinion. Schools need principled, self-critical governors. The tiny minority of bigoted, self-important governors do untold damage to the reputation of schools and governing bodies alike.

2   What Motivates You

Task 2
Your
Motivation

Think of a time when you really got involved in something in a big way, giving lots of time, attention and commitment to it. Why did you do it? What did you get out of it?

Identify the kinds of things that motivate you.

Indicate the degree to which the following incentives motivate you. Score each one on a scale of 1 - 5, where 1 = highly motivating and 5 = not motivating at all.

Motivation	Grade
● Money/material reward	
● Praise - public	
● Praise - private	
● Fear of failure	
● Sense of personal achievement; improvement on previous personal best	
● Competition against one or more than one; the chance to beat someone else	
● Promotion in your job	
● Others' high opinion	
● Self-esteem	
● Contribution to the general good; altruism/making other people happy	
● Self-protection	
● Others: (add any that matter to you that I have not included)	

Highlight your top five motivating factors.

Understanding what motivates us in any situation can often be very difficult. It is seldom simple. There are often a number of different factors, some more influential than others.

For example, let us imagine that Mr Wright, a recently retired garage mechanic, chooses to become a school governor in order to give something back to the local community which he feels has rewarded and supported him in his career. His prime motivation may well be altruistic and community-minded. At the same time, he may feel that governorship will also provide him with a sense of purpose and self-worth.

Self-protection and self-interest, enlightened or otherwise, could influence his decision. The role may also offer him new or continued friendships and a chance to go on learning.

Personal development could be a driving force. He may feel that such a public role will maintain his position of respect in the town and being appointed by his local County Councillor enhances his self-esteem. It may be that he does not like one or two of the other governors and sees this as a chance to get even with them or thwart their plans, so competition, rivalry or envy might be other factors.

Mr Wright may or may not be aware of all the possible motivations underlying his apparently benevolent action. Some may be positive, some negative. Unless he looks honestly within himself, he may never know the answers. Others, however, will read many different meanings into his apparently straightforward decision, perhaps attributing an even wider range of motives to the poor man! Once he begins working as a governor, what motivates him at any one time will be a mixture of every factor described above, as well as new ones which emerge in the fullness of time.

Motivations can conflict with each other and change during the time we are involved with a given project or activity. Our motivation changes with each new situation and will vary at different times in our lives and according to other personal circumstances, such as our feelings of security, happiness, self-worth and so on. Some judicious self-analysis can be of great value. When you are considering becoming a school governor, having a clearer idea about why you're doing it (and what will help you to keep doing it when the going gets tougher) will help you to make a sound decision and a success of the role. In *Section Two*, I will ask you to identify the reasons why you became a governor. The initial self-analysis you have just completed will help you to be clear about your answers.

3   Your Personal Goals

Task 3
Your Goals

Imagine yourself at 10, 15 and 20 years old. At each stage, list/describe/draw how you saw yourself in the future.

Repeat the activity, basing it on how you see yourself now.

Look forward five years from now. Visualise and describe yourself: your home life and close relationships; your possessions; your work. Make sure you use only the present tense.

Look back to today and list the significant "milestone" events that brought about this new situation. Add a date to each one.

- *Which of your dreams, visions or goals came true? Why did they come true and others did not?*

- *What do you still want to achieve; be like; improve in yourself?*

It often feels strange to attempt to be this explicit about our ambitions and dreams. It's probably easy enough to think like this about our work or career, but the days of "I want to be a train driver when I grow up" are gone. Not the dream, of course, but the concept of a secure job for life. Career breaks, redundancy, "portfolio working", unemployment, "downshifting": choices confront us; events overtake us; the future becomes less and less predictable. So, even in an area where it might seem reasonable to try to plan a future, it is getting harder to do so.

Our lives should not be - cannot be - planned, should they? Don't we tend to worry about people who have their lives mapped out in front of them? We know that life is uncertain, unpredictable. We have to be adaptable, resilient, optimistic in order to cope with all that life throws at us.

All that is true. But we still have our ideas of the future, and it is not unreasonable to think about where we want to be or what we want to be like in the future. Finding a meaning and a purpose in life involves consideration of the future. If we have an idea of what we want to change or achieve, we can plan.

If you have bought this book you are likely to be somebody who believes that service to others is a moral obligation, that we are members one of another. Voluntary work is usually undertaken by people whose personal goals include the search for a quality of life which is not measured in material and selfish rewards. Wanting to give something back to the community; wanting to contribute to the greater good of society; wanting to help build a better future combines values, motivations and goals. It is this impulse to make a difference which may well have led you to becoming, or wanting to become, a governor in the first place. Remembering this motive helps to sustain commitment during the difficult times.

4   Sources of Personal Authority

In any kind of group - whether it be a family, a sports team or an office team -   it is quite common for the experienced member, let alone the new, to feel in a weak position. One feels unable to influence the development of the group, its behaviour or its policies.

Such a feeling is equally true of governing bodies. Whilst no governor has any power as an individual, since powers and responsibilities belong only to the governing body as a whole, it seldom feels like this. As with any other kind of group, there are degrees of influence distributed amongst the membership. Some members of the group tend to dominate the rest, using a variety of conscious or unconscious methods of getting their own way. Yet potentially, each member of the group could influence its work and development, so why do some members have more influence than others? To find the answer to this conundrum, carry out *Task 4*.

Task 4
Sources of
Personal
Authority

> Think of a number of different people you know who in your eyes are natural leaders: i.e. people whose ideas are respected and followed; people whom others will follow.
>
> Why is this?
> From where do these people get their authority?
>
> Write down your ideas.
>
> Think of a situation in which you took the lead, or in which others followed your lead, in some way. If this has happened to you, what gave you that sense of authority?
>
> Write down your ideas.

The Effective School Governor

Consider how you behave in any number of group situations: e.g. family reunion; work team; sports/quiz team; crisis situation; planning group.

How do you influence the behaviour of the group and affect what happens?
Write down your ideas.

People have varying degrees of personal authority. They may demonstrate different degrees of personal authority in different situations. Your source of personal authority can be derived from:

- Your role or position
- Your control of resources
- Your expertise or knowledge
- Your charisma or personal authority
- Your physical power

Task 4 will have helped you to think about some aspects of this subject. To explore it a little further, write down the answers to the questions in *Task 5*.

Task 5
Checking the Sources of Your Authority

Which **groups** do you belong to?

What **roles** do you play or what position do you hold in each group?

What **resources** do you control?

How **physically** powerful are you?

What **expertise** or **specialist knowledge** do you have?

What **charisma** or **personal authority** can you exercise?

I am confident that you will have identified a number of potential, if not actual, sources of authority. If we feel powerless to influence any group of which we are a member, it is not because we have no source of authority, but rather that either we have not identified it, or we know what it is and choose not to use it. Incubating a sense of powerlessness or learned helplessness can be both a comfort (excusing us from involvement in difficult decisions, for example) or, paradoxically, a form of power, allowing us to manipulate others into doing work on our behalf.

Honest self-analysis in this area can be painful but is, I would argue, very important. It is no use having good ideas if you cannot persuade colleagues to take them on board. Recognition of the fact that, however inexperienced you may be as a governor, you have a sound foundation for your personal authority, means that you can play an effective part from the word go, rather than waiting for someone else to grant you permission to be involved. It also means that you can more readily identify in others the source of their authority, enabling you to challenge or enhance it as appropriate.

In *Section Three*, I will return to this theme and show how it can be applied to a governing body.

5   Your Areas of Interest, Skills and Abilities, and Personal Qualities

It's important to be clear about these areas. Most of us tend to be modest about ourselves, even in private! Take a cool, objective look and evaluate yourself by completing *Task 6*, below. Ask someone who knows you well to do the same for you and then compare the results.

Task 6

Your Interests, Skills and Personal Qualities

Complete this table. Some sample answers are included for your guidance.

Interest	Skill or Ability	Personal Quality
Local history	Parenting	Sense of humour
Football	Juggling	Calm under pressure
Music	Desk top publishing	

1. Do it yourself
2. Get a friend or family member to do it for you

Interest	Skill or ability	Personal quality

Compare the results and complete a single table containing all the details you believe most accurately describe your areas of interests, skills and personal qualities.

It can sometimes be a bit of a surprise when you see your completed list. It's easy to forget certain skills, interests and achievements in a busy life. We acquire new skills and abilities all the time and, unless we need to apply them to our immediate situations, we tend to forget them, although, like riding a bicycle, we seldom lose the ability once mastered.

Being an effective governor calls upon a wide range of talents, skills and knowledge. It may not be apparent at first how some of your attributes might be applied, but you should remain open-minded about the possibilities, and seek to make full use of them as you learn more and more about the work and its demands. You may not be able to use all your talents as a governor, but you will be surprised at the many demands of the job and how some of your "forgotten skills" may be needed!

During *Section Two*, we will return to your responses to the tasks on *Section One*. We will attempt to find out how you can use what you have learned to support your work as a governor. Try to keep a clear sense of yourself as a person as you proceed through the rest of the book. Remember, it is the uniqueness of your qualities as a human being which underpin the way you carry out your governor responsibilities.

Section Two

Your Effectiveness as an Individual Governor

Having carried out some self-evaluation in *Section One,* and identified amongst other things, your values, skills and interests, you are now in a good position to explore ways in which you might apply what you've learned to your role as a school governor. I shall assume you have a working knowledge of the governor's job, but if you are unsure of this, you can refer to the Appendix (pages 81-83) to find a list of roles and responsibilities.

Your time is limited, even if your commitment is total. Being effective in the role involves a recognition of what is possible and ensuring that your energies are directed at the things that really matter. In *Section Three* I will take you through the issues associated with working as part of the team of governors. *Section Two,* however, looks in some detail at how you can prepare yourself to make the most of what you can offer as an individual.

In this section you will:

- ☛ **Assess your motivation as a governor**
- ☛ **Assess your goals as a governor**
- ☛ **Analyse and recognise the limits to your commitment as a governor**
- ☛ **Examine ways of using your interests, skills and abilities and personal qualities as a governor**
- ☛ **Consider your training and development needs as a governor and how to meet them**
- ☛ **Explore your induction as a new governor**

It is common to find, as a new governor, that you feel very ignorant and lacking in confidence about the contributions you can make. After all, what can you offer? What do you know about that could be useful to your colleagues? Even months or years into the role, you may still feel this way.

There are, in reality, at least four kinds of ignorance, and it's worth bearing these in mind as we work through the rest of this book:

- What you know you don't know
- What you don't know you don't know
- What you think you know but you don't
- What you think you don't know but you do

The last of these is the one to keep at the forefront of your mind. Governors are meant to be lay people with no special inside knowledge of education. They are there to ask the questions that an ordinary person would and should ask. At the same time, they bring to the job a range of experience and knowledge of the world beyond education that is often far wider, when taken collectively, than that of the teachers in the school. They have a real role to play in representing the community served by the school.

1 Your Motivation as a Governor

Why on earth did I become a governor?

Q It's a question most of us ask ourselves at one stage or another in our career in school governance. This is what one group of governors told me:

"I'd been a teacher and I wanted to keep in touch with education...and keep up to date with what's happening."

Carol McCaw

"I wanted to make a contribution to the local community."

Roger Griffiths

"I saw it as part of my personal and professional development, to get involved in the strategic planning of the governing body."

Colin Green, Primary Head

"I wanted to contribute to my children's school and felt I had something I could offer."

Lorraine Billis

"It was out of a real sense of gratitude for the good and happy education my children were receiving and wanting to give something back to the school."

Ruth Richards

"I had been a parent helper and a member of the PTA for quite a few years but now I wanted to get involved at the policy-making level."

Gail Grant

from **Governing Schools Effectively Right from the Start**, *CD Rom.*
(Wiltshire County Council, 1997)

You may well recognise one or more of these reasons. It's possible that there were several different reasons. It is worth spending a moment or two thinking this through in order to be clear about it.

Task 7

Your Motivation as a Governor

Look back at your assessment of what motivates you. (*Task 2 on page 16*)

Which, if any, of those factors motivated you to become a governor? Add a tick against any which apply.

Which continue to motivate you? Add an asterisk in each case.

List any additional motivations you may have that you're aware of.

Indicate, with a cross, any of your original motivations which were not borne out by your experience.

Being an effective governor means being a member of a group. Research has shown that people use groups for one or more of the following purposes:

> A means of satisfying their social or affiliation needs; to belong to something or to share in something.
>
> A means of establishing a self-concept. Most people find it easier to define themselves in terms of their relationship to others, as members of a role-set with a role in that set.
>
> A means of gaining help and support to carry out their particular objectives, which may or may not be the same as the organisation's objectives.
>
> A means of sharing and helping in a common activity or purpose which may be making a product, or carrying out a job, or having fun, or giving help, or creating something.
>
> ...these purposes often overlap. They may also conflict...
>
> from **Understanding Organizations,** Handy C, (Penguin Books, 1993)

You might choose to check your motivations against this list, too.

You may have found that there is a great deal of similarity between what motivates you generally and what motivates you as a governor. If this is the case, then you will undoubtedly feel comfortable with the demands of the role, and be in a strong position to contribute effectively and gain personal benefit from your commitment.

Where there are some differences, this probably does not matter, since you are unlikely to find a perfect match. There may be a problem if the discrepancy is too great and there is little correlation. This might suggest that you misunderstood the role or were misled about it by someone else. If there is little to motivate you in the work, there is no point carrying on. Sadly, some governors find this to be the case and feel that the only honourable course of action open to them is to resign.

It may be that you are a reader who is thinking about becoming a governor. Working through these tasks may lead you to discover that the role is not for you. If that is the case then I feel I will have done a good job. This is not because there is a never-ending supply of excellent governors ready to step into the breach, but it would be doubly disheartening for you - and your governing body - to have to go through a painful learning process of discovering that you were not right for the job, and that the whole process of filling the vacancy had to begin again.

I suspect that if you had the motivation to buy this book in the first place, you are not likely to fall into this latter category, and I'm confident that you will find much to motivate you in your work as a governor.

2   Your Goals as a Governor

In *Section One Task 3* (page 17) we looked at your personal goals. Look at these again and try the same exercise as we did in *Task 7* (page 24) in relation to your motivations.

Having a clear set of goals as a governor is probably easier than having "life goals". It is very helpful to remind yourself of your goals as a governor when you feel you're losing your way in the work. This is a common experience. It is easy to become bogged down in some of the minutiae of meetings, legislation and very specific problems needing a solution. We all need to "gain height" from time to time; to gain perspective on where we are, on what's been happening and on where we're going. Renewing your focus is essential. Being clear about your goals is one good way of providing yourself with a sense of direction. So let's be clear about your goals as a governor.

The next task is to list what you will have achieved by the end of your (first) four years in office. For example, you might want to have learned more about:

the curriculum
finance or personnel matters
becoming a successful Chairperson
developing a good relationship with the teachers and the Head
achieving accreditation for your work as a governor.

Task 8
Your Goals as
a Governor

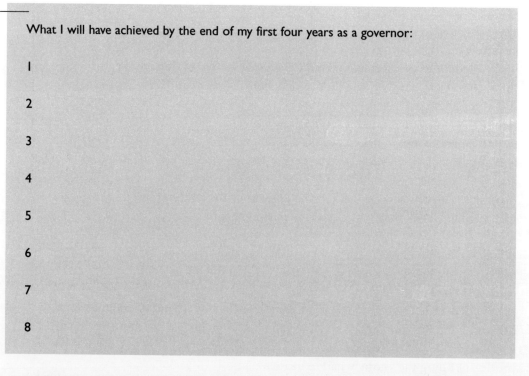

What I will have achieved by the end of my first four years as a governor:

1

2

3

4

5

6

7

8

As with School Development Planning, a process in which you are - or will be - involved as a governor, establishing goals is vital to a sense of achievement. They will take time to achieve, and that achievement needs to be planned for, since they won't be achieved by accident. Writing them down is a good starting point, but think through now what actions you will need to take, when you will take them, what resources you will need (especially time!), who else might be involved, and when and how you will review progress.

This kind of planning can be difficult, especially since it involves anticipating the future, so it's worth asking a friend or colleague to talk it through with you. The more specific you can be, the more likely you are to achieve your goals. Some of the remaining tasks in this section will also provide prompts and guidelines for this process.

3   Analysing and Recognising the Limitations to Your Commitment as a Governor

It is a simple fact that there is never enough time to do the job of governor properly. If you're familiar with the full list of governors' responsibilities, you will know how impossible the whole thing seems. People thinking about becoming a governor always want to know, quite rightly, how much time it will take. It's hard to answer this one because the time commitment varies so much according to the time of year; the particular circumstances of the school; the levels of commitment of fellow governors; whether you are the Chair of governors; and many other factors. Particular events, such as the appointment of a new headteacher, can place sudden and urgent demands upon your time, whereas school holiday periods tend to see a quietening down of activity. Here are some comments from governors:

> "On average, I'm likely to be in the school for some of most days in the week, but probably for no more than one hour at a time."
>> *Rev. David Seymour*

> "About half a day in school per week when it's busy."
>> *Colin Minto*

> "Two or three evenings per week, involving a couple of hours per evening."
>> *Richard Millard*

> "At least three or four hours per week."
>> *Ruth Richards*

> *from* **Governing Schools Effectively Right from the Start,** *CD Rom (Wiltshire County Council, 1997)*

You may already be clear about the amount of time you are prepared to give to being a governor, but if you want to avoid it taking over your life, it's a good idea to set yourself some limits. It's hard to stick to these, of course, especially when something really important has to be sorted out, but unless you impose some limits yourself, there is no end to the amount of time you could spend on being a governor. In many ways, it could easily be a full-time job.

A common feeling amongst hard-working governors is that they are not doing the job well enough. They feel guilty that they are not giving even more time to it. The problem is that the job could easily occupy every waking hour, so no matter how much time they give, it will never be enough. The secret is to ensure that whatever time you can devote to the work is used effectively, that it is not wasted in pointless tasks or meandering discussions. For me, this is what being an effective governor is all about: *using your limited time to maximum effect.*

Then there are your other commitments such as your family, work, home, leisure activities and all the other things that occupy your mind and time. Your commitment as a governor needs to be set against these necessary demands, so that you don't promise yourself to give more than you are able. The following task will help you determine a realistic level of commitment against which you can occasionally check the amount of time and effort you're giving up.

Task 9

Your Commitment as a Governor

How many hours per week, on average, do you think you give (or are prepared to give) to being a governor? (This includes attendance at full governing body meetings and any committees, by the way.)

I am prepared to give an average of .... hours per week to being a governor.

How many hours per week, roughly, do you spend on:

Your work _____ hours

Your family commitments _____ hours

Your leisure activities _____ hours

Housework/home maintenance _____ hours

Sleeping _____ 56 hours

Other _____ hours

_____ hours

_____ hours

Total _____ hours

Total hours available _____ **168** hours

Total hours remaining _____ hours

Now compare the time you thought you could commit to what is actually remaining, once everything else is accounted for. You may have a nasty shock! Whatever the outcome, you should now have a realistic idea of what's possible, so that you won't over-commit yourself. You may wish, of course, to revaluate how you spend your time: that's up to you.

What, though, is your commitment as a governor? The DfEE's **"Guidance on Good Governance"** lists the following:

Each governor:

- Participates in the work of the governing body, for example serving on committees and working groups; this includes preparing for meetings, attending meetings, contributing to discussion, and taking part in agreed action after meetings.

- Gets to know the school and becomes familiar with it as a result of discussions with the headteacher and staff, reading relevant papers, visiting the school and taking part in school events.

- Tries to increase his or her ability to contribute to the work of the governing body by taking part in available training and other opportunities to develop knowledge, skills and understanding.

- Helps new governors to understand their role and to make a full contribution.

- Seeks at all times to promote the best interests of the school and the education of its pupils.

- Declares personal or pecuniary interests and

- Avoids using his or her position as a governor for personal gain or the gain of other outside parties, or to promote the interests of his or her own children to the detriment of others.

from **Guidance on Good Governance**, *DfEE (The Stationery Office Ltd., 1996, Crown Copyright)*

This, I feel, is a very useful *aide-mémoire* for any governor. If all governors lived up to it equally well, headteachers would never have any justification for complaining about their governing body! Part of the purpose of this book is to provide practical help to enable you to live up to these commitments.

4 Using Your Interests, Skills and Personal Qualities

As I suggested in *Section One*, the extensive responsibilities and activities of governing bodies demand a phenomenal range of knowledge, skills and aptitudes. No single member of the team will possess all of - or even, perhaps, more than one of - the required attributes of the effective governor. What matters is that your governing body should ensure that you and your personal resources are used to the maximum benefit of the governing body and the school as a whole. In order to do this effectively, you and your colleagues need to be clear about what you can offer and how it can best be used.

In *Section One, Task 6* (page 20), you and a second person evaluated your interests, skills and personal qualities. You will need to return to that list in order to complete the next task. In this new task, you are asked to match your interests, skills and personal qualities against the requirements of governorship.

Task 10

Using Your
Interests, Skills
and Personal
Qualities

Alongside each aspect of the governor's work (listed in the Appendix) and the skills demanded, tick those to which you feel you could contribute. Add any notes you think might be useful.

If you're already a governor:

which of your interests, skills and personal qualities are being used?

which are being underused or not used at all?

what will you do to ensure that as many as possible are used to maximum effect?

Add your comments in the appropriate column.

Governor's responsibilities, roles and personal qualities	Relevant interests, skills and personal qualities	Notes
Areas of responsibility		
Financial Matters		
Curriculum Matters		
Premises Matters		
Personnel Issues		

The Effective School Governor

Governor's responsibilities, roles and personal qualities	Relevant interests, skills and personal qualities	Notes
Roles		
Supporting the School		
Accountability		
Executive		
Monitoring		
Steering		

Governor's responsibilities, roles and personal qualities	Relevant interests, skills and personal qualities	Notes
What schools want from you		
An Interest in Education		
Commitment to your School		
Tolerance and the Ability to Work with Others		
Patience		
Enthusiasm		
Willingness to Learn		
Involvement in the Life of the School		
Openness and Democracy		

I expect you found some of these aspects easier to respond to than others, especially if you are unsure what some categories involve. You might choose to add to the analysis as you continue to develop as a governor and come to understand better what each category means. It's unlikely that you will have found it possible to respond in detail to every category, and I would not expect you to.

What is important is to have a *clear and honest understanding of what you can offer,* so that you can avoid being under-or misused as a member of your governing body and its committees. This understanding can also help to pinpoint areas where you might seek development, either now or in the future.

5   Training and Development

As you completed *Task 10* (pages 30-32), you probably identified at least a few areas of governance in which you lack expertise, knowledge or skills. I would be very surprised if you did not! A common response is to seek appropriate training in order to overcome your "deficiency". Training for governors is not compulsory. However, in **"Governing Bodies and Effective Schools"**, the authors identified the features of effective governing bodies (summarised on page 39 of this book). The final feature listed was *Training and Development.*

> To help their schools most effectively, governing bodies need to take their own development seriously. They should consider their training and support needs carefully, and be prepared to allocate funds for external courses, visits to other schools, or training for the whole governing body.
>
> *from* **Governing Bodies and Effective Schools**, *Barber M, Stoll L, Mortimore P, Hillman J, (DfEE/Ofsted/BIS 1995, Crown Copyright)*

Despite this, there are plenty of governors who have never received any training in the work and still do a good job. It may not be their fault that they have not been trained, since the provision of good quality governor training is very patchy, as the Chief Inspector of Schools pointed out in his annual report on inspections carried out in 1994-5:

> Governors' training is often haphazard, and even with funding included in the overall school improvement grant, some governors remain understandably but short-sightedly reluctant to spend money on their own development.
>
> *from* **The Annual Report of Her Majesty's Chief Inspector of Schools: Standards and Quality in Education 1994-5**, *Woodhead C, (The Stationery Office Ltd, 1996 Crown Copyright)*

The time issue raises its ugly head again in this context. Good quality training takes time in whatever form it's provided. A governor with a full time job cannot attend day courses, for obvious reasons. In some cases, the employer is willing to give paid time off for employees to carry out their duties. In fact, employers are obliged by law to give "reasonable time off" for the work, but they don't have to pay you. Evening courses are an alternative, but for some people it's not the best learning time in the day, and there are the usual competing demands that we looked at earlier. Weekend courses might appeal to some but, again, it takes real commitment to give up valuable free time to attend.

Of course, governor training can be provided in other forms: literature; audiotapes; videotapes and CD-ROM. In most cases, you should be able to find some form of training that suits your circumstances.

Task 11

Training Needs

In what areas do you feel you need and want training, information or development?

Look back at *Task 10* (pages 30-32) and remind yourself of the areas in which you feel you lack the necessary knowledge or skills. Using the table below, make a list of them and then prioritise them by assigning a number to each, where I equals top priority, 2 equals second priority and so on.

Next, identify whether what you need is information or skills (or an alternative form of knowledge or ability).

Finally, identify whether you could find what you need from a book or other source of information, or whether it demands active training.

Training/Information Required	Priority Rating	Knowledge or Skills?	Training or Reading?

Getting Access to Training

There are three common sources of training and information about school governance.

First, at the *local* level, there is the school itself. The Head, the staff and other governors are a resource to be used, especially by the new governor. Of course, it's important to choose your moment. We're all busy people and some enquiries need time to consider and prepare an answer. So make an appointment to talk to the person who can help you, especially if it's a full answer you're looking for. Visiting the school and the classroom is a very important way of seeing at first hand what it is you're meant to be governing! We'll look at this in more detail in *Section Three*.

The Effective School Governor

At the level of your *local authority*, there will usually be some form of training provided by your Local Education Authority or LEA. In "**School Governors: A Guide to the Law**" it says:

> The Local Education Authority provides the training it thinks necessary for governors to carry out their duties effectively. They must do this free of charge to each governor. Most Local Education Authorities offer governor training to schools under a package which the governing body pays a subscription for.
>
> *from* **School Governors: A Guide to the Law**, *DfEE (The Stationery Office Ltd., 1997 Crown Copyright)*

The extent and quality of this training varies enormously. If you're lucky, you will find you have access to a full range of support services, including a training menu or programme; individual governing body development; a resources library; distance learning materials and so on. At worst, you may be given a pile of documents to read.

Other providers exist, too, such as Diocesan Authorities who provide training for governors of controlled and aided schools.

At the *national* level there are a number of organisations providing training and conferences, including the National Association of Governors and Managers (NAGM) and the Institution of School and College Governors (ISCG):

The National Association of Governors and Managers (NAGM)
Suite 36-38
21 Bennetts Hill
Birmingham B2 5QP
0121 643 5787

The Institution of School and College Governors (ISCG).
Avondale School
Sirdar Road
London W11 4EE
0171 229 0200

Learning Styles
It's very important to think about your preferred learning style when you're contemplating training. Some people prefer to sit quietly on their own, reading up about something they want to know more about. Others prefer the interaction with other people that comes with attending a training event. Others prefer the possibilities offered by information technology, including the Internet and CD-ROM. People learn most effectively in different ways. Think about the best learning experiences you have had and ask yourself the question such as:

"How did I learn that skill?"

"Why did that learning come so easily to me?"

It may be that you can identify the ways in which you learn best and then seek similar sorts of training and learning to suit your personality.

One of the unalterable laws of school governance is that there is always more to know than there is time in which to know it. Even having prioritised your training and learning needs, there's no point in rushing to complete your development at the earliest opportunity. Take your time and plan your learning over the four years or more of your term(s) of office.

Whilst the whole emphasis of this book is on the governor as an individual - and I have been writing about your accessing training as an individual - I believe the most effective developmental work you can do is as part of the team. There is a lot of invaluable reading and training you can do on your own. It can help you enormously to be a more effective governor.

However, I often come across the plight of the keen governor who is desperate but unable to influence the behaviour and knowledge of her or his governing body, simply because his/hers is a lone voice. Even if only one other person can train with you, it's worth it because you stand a much better chance of "cascading" the learning to colleagues as a pair. Even better is the situation where maybe half the governors can attend training. Better still is where the training comes to you as a complete governing body. It has been my experience that a day's developmental work - with the teachers, support staff and governors joining together - is the most powerful and effective training of all.

Finally, keep a record of your training and development. It only takes a couple of minutes and can be a very helpful reminder of what you did and when and how you did it. Ideally, the whole governing body will keep a collective record. The record would include the titles and dates of the training undertaken, together with a comment on its usefulness or otherwise. You might also consider noting how you can share your learning with colleagues and, perhaps, what positive difference the training makes after six months or so.

6   Your Induction

An effective induction process is central to your early success as a governor. You can be effective without one - but it's much harder and takes longer. It's perfectly possible to spend a whole year out of your four year term learning how to make your contribution, left only to yourself.

Although it is now more common for governing bodies to have developed an effective induction policy, not every governing body has yet done so and so you may find you receive little or no induction. Please don't give up if things don't happen as they should. To some extent, you may feel able to take the initiative here. Once established as a governor, you might be willing and able to take a lead in developing an induction policy for those who follow you. Often it's the most recent "victim" who is in the best position to rectify the faults. What follows is an outline of what a good induction might include.

What are the principles of induction?

- Induction should be seen as an investment, leading to more effective governance and retention of governors.

- It should be welcoming, informative and helpful in getting a feel for the role.

- It should promote the partnership between governing bodies, teachers, parents, pupils and the local education authority (where appropriate).

- It might offer a generic introduction - covering a broad range of topics - which can then lead on to specific areas of responsibility.

Who does what and when?

It is a good idea to share out the various tasks involved in the induction process between governors, headteacher and clerk, with a clear, relevant and fair allocation of responsibilities to appropriate people.

Everyone involved needs to have an agreed programme, with dates and times, in order to avoid both duplication and omission of key elements of the process.

Task 12
What does the New Governor Need to Know?

Look at each item in the table below. Rate how important each piece of information or document was or would have been to you as a new governor. If you're not yet a governor, you could still estimate the priority order. Give a 1 to your highest priority - and so on.

In the *When?* column, note down when you think is the best time to receive this information or document. For example, you might decide that the best time to receive the plan of the school is before your first meeting.

Information/Document	Priority	When?
A plan of the school		
The annual report to parents		
The school development plan and Ofsted summary report and action plan		
An induction pack or programme		
Guidelines on visiting the school		
Calendar of governors' meetings, including committees		
Brief description of how meetings are conducted		
A list of staff and their responsibilities		
An events calendar		
Recent school newsletters		
Outlines of current issues relating to personnel, curriculum, finances, premises		
Where to get help		
Description of committees with associated terms of reference		
Local Education Authority Governor Support: course programmes		
Summary of school policies		
A prospectus		

This exercise can also be used as a personal checklist to monitor what you receive(d) as a new governor.

Of course, how useful it all is will depend on the quality of the documents themselves. Schools and governing bodies vary enormously in the time and effort they put into their documentation. One area in which a new governor can have an immediate impact is in improving, if it's necessary, the design, content and user-friendliness of informative literature. (Don't just do this without consulting your fellow governors though, or it could cause a great deal of offence!)

Making contact: the human touch, the smiling face and the helping hand!

Induction is not only about documents and piles of information. You might try some or all of the following strategies:

- ☛ An informal, friendly talk with the headteacher, followed by a more extended visit and tour of the school - in the working day, if possible.

- ☛ A phone call from the chair, welcoming the newcomer and giving an update on current issues.

- ☛ One governor acts as mentor, starting with a cup of tea and a chat. He or she accompanies the newcomer to the first meeting and lends helpful books and materials.

- ☛ Have a social gathering before the governing body meeting, with teachers invited.

At the first meeting attended by the newcomer:

- ☛ Introduce all governors, informally, including brief background details.

- ☛ Wear name badges.

- ☛ Explain all acronyms and jargon (this could be a long meeting!).

- ☛ Explain the context of each major agenda item.

- ☛ Ask the newcomer to join a committee but reassure him/her that there is no expectation that he/she will play a leading role just yet.

Review of Section 2

This section has asked you to look hard at yourself and what you can offer as an individual. If you were not aware of these things before, you will now have:

- ☛ A realistic and positive view of why you're a governor.

- ☛ What you are aiming to achieve.

- ☛ What you can and cannot offer in terms of time, skills and experience.

- ☛ What you still need to learn.

- ☛ What you need to make an effective start in the role.

So far, so good. But being a governor entails working with others. This can be frustrating - or an essential support for your individual commitment. Operating to maximum effectiveness within a group is quite a challenge and demands a range of skills, knowledge and attitudes which we will explore in *Section Three*.

Section Three

Your Effectiveness as a Member of Your Governing Body

Fulfilling an effective role in any group requires a careful balancing of one's individuality with the character of the group as a whole. Governing bodies are full of different kinds of people from a wide variety of backgrounds. The age-range can be enormous, the skills, experience and attitudes of members may be radically different, and each member's understanding of what it takes to work well in a group may also differ considerably. In some ways, it can be a recipe for disaster.

However, in other respects, this diversity can offer a very valuable resource to the school and to individual members of the group. In addition, the membership seldom remains stable for long, so the character of the group changes regularly and sometimes radically.

In order to be a truly effective governor, it is vital to have some understanding of how groups work and how individuals behave in groups. This section looks at these issues and offers some practical ways of flourishing within a disparate group of fellow volunteers.

In this section we will look at the following:

> ☞ **Can a governing body become an effective team?: the flaws of governance; inadequate prescriptions; towards a new governance**
> ☞ **Roles in the team**
> ☞ **Finding your role**
> ☞ **Your effectiveness in meetings**
> ☞ **Committee work**
> ☞ **Visiting the school and the classroom**
> ☞ **Developing partnerships**
> ☞ **Succession planning and continuity**

1 Can a Governing Body Become an Effective Team?

The features of an effective governing body have been identified and have become nearly as well known as the features of effective schools:

- Working as a team
- Good relationship with the headteacher
- Effective time management and delegation
- Effective meetings
- Knowing the school
- Training and development

from **Governing Bodies and Effective Schools**, *Barber M, Stoll L, Mortimore P, Hillman J (DfEE/Ofsted/BIS 1995, Crown Copyright)*

Before considering the effectiveness of your governing body as a team, you need to remember the aim of school governance which is stated firmly in **"Lessons In Teamwork"**:

Q | The main aim of a governing body is to maintain and improve the standards of achievement in its school.

from **Lessons In Teamwork: How School Governing Bodies Can Become More Effective**, *Audit Commission/Ofsted (The Stationery Office Ltd.,1995.*

"Governing Bodies and Effective Schools" lists three main roles for the governing body in raising standards and improving schools:

Q | 1. To provide a strategic view

The governing body has important powers and duties but limited time and resources. So it should focus on where it can add most value - that is, in helping to decide the school's strategy for improvement so that its pupils learn most effectively and achieve the highest standards.

The governing body should help to set, and keep under review, the broad framework within which the headteacher and staff should run the school. In all its work, the governing body should focus on the key issues of raising standards of achievement, establishing high expectations and promoting effective teaching and learning.

2. To act as a critical friend

The governing body also provides the headteacher and staff with support, advice and information, drawing on its members' knowledge and experience. In these ways the governing body acts as a critical friend to the school.

Critical in the sense of its responsibility for monitoring and evaluating the school's effectiveness, asking challenging questions, and pressing for improvement. A friend because it exists to promote the interests of the school and its pupils.

3. To ensure accountability

The governing body is responsible for ensuring good quality education in the school. The headteacher and staff report to the governing body on the school's performance. It is not the role of governors simply to rubber-stamp every decision of the headteacher.

The governing body has a right to discuss, question and refine proposals - while always respecting the professional roles of the headteacher and other staff, and their responsibilities for the management of the school. In its turn the governing body answers for its actions, above all to parents and the wider local community for the school's overall performance.

from **Governing Bodies and Effective Schools**, *Barber M, Stoll L, Mortimore P, Hillman J (DfEE/Ofsted/BIS 1995, Crown Copyright)*

These three roles are very challenging for most, if not all, governing bodies. Many governors take on the work because they want to support the school, which is a very good reason for doing it. Schools need all the support they can get. However, the support role is fairly comfortable and relatively easy to accomplish. Being a *critical friend* poses more of a challenge. **"Excellence In Schools"** (DfEE; The Stationery Office Ltd; July 1997) encourages governing bodies to "challenge the expectations of the headteacher and staff as well as providing support". This theme runs through the three roles described above, but as yet, few governors of my acquaintance have the confidence (let alone the objective data) which would enable them to do this job. It will be a major aspect of the development of the governing body's work in the near future.

One vital aspect of governing body effectiveness, then, is related to the extent to which it accomplishes the three roles. That is not the *primary* focus of this section, although I will refer to some elements of these three roles.

Another equally vital aspect is how effectively the governing body behaves as a group and how well it conducts its business. As an individual member of the group, you can play a significant role in increasing its effectiveness, however good or bad it is. *Remember that you don't have to be ill to get better!* It is this aspect that we will consider here.

The first feature of an effective governing body listed in **"Governing Bodies and Effective Schools"** is:

> **Working as a team**
>
> Building an effective team requires regular attendance and energetic commitment from all governors. It means making use of what each governor has to offer, sharing the workload, give-and-take on individual issues, respect for colleagues and their differing opinions, and loyalty to final decisions.
>
> *from* **Governing Bodies and Effective Schools**, *Barber M, Stoll L, Mortimore P, Hillman J, (DfEE/Ofsted/BIS 1995, Crown Copyright)*

I couldn't disagree with a word of this, but there is a simple logistical problem here. The development of effective teamwork depends upon regular contact with one another, possibly on a daily basis. Governing bodies meet infrequently, perhaps twice a term, maybe five or six times in any one year. This represents quite a commitment, but it does not involve frequent contact between all governors. Such meetings tend to be fairly formal and not especially conducive to team development. Governing bodies are not in the habit of reviewing the process as well as the content of their meetings.

Individual governors also meet each other in committees and these meetings are usually more informal and can be more creative. However, they can work against the development of the whole team, especially if one committee feels itself to be more important than the others.

In smaller primary schools it is often the case that at least some of the governors know each other reasonably well. This can aid the development of productive working relationships and team spirit. It can just as easily lend itself to factionalism and splits. Some of the most extreme crises within governing bodies happen in small village communities where the governing body contains representatives of the opposing sides of village politics. In this sort of hothouse atmosphere, the proper work of the governing body is overtaken by power struggles that have little or nothing to do with the children in the school. Even where a team develops, its continuity is threatened by the four-year changeover of members.

It could be argued, then, that it is unrealistic to expect your governing body to become an effective team. Nevertheless, it's reasonable to expect to find some aspects of good teamwork in the way your governing body works. You can play a vital role in helping this to develop.

Does your governing body ever consider its effectiveness as a team? Do you ask yourselves why you do things the way you do? Could your meetings be more efficient and more focused on the curriculum and pupil achievement? There are many facets of this and, as I wrote in the introduction to the book, there are some excellent materials available to help you to self-evaluate as a group. Please refer to the list of resources at the end of the book for details. I would recommend Michael Creese's **"Effective Governors, Effective Schools: Developing the Partnership"** (Fulton, 1995) as a sound starting point.

Where a governing body has undertaken any degree of self-review, however, it may well have discovered some of the common *flaws of governance*. In his book, **"Boards That Make a Difference"** (Jossey-Bass, 1990), John Carver identified the common flaws of governance.

Task 13

Flaws of Governance

Assess your governing body against these common flaws. Tick the "Yes, we do this" column as appropriate. Add any ideas you may have for solving this problem in the "Solution" column.

Flaw	Yes, we do this	Solution
Too much time spent on trivial matters		
Short term thinking, planning and perspectives		
Reacting to events rather than anticipating and planning for them		
Rehashing and redoing things unnecessarily		
Leaky accountability		
Authority diffuse: a lack of clarity over who is responsible for what		

from **Boards That Make a Difference**, *Carver J (Jossey-Bass, 1990)*

The Effective School Governor

Your solutions may prove effective if you can implement them and will almost certainly have to involve the whole governing body. Unfortunately, Carver discovered that many prescriptions have been tried before by other governing bodies and have been found to be inadequate. These were the inadequate prescriptions he found, in summary:

- More involvement
- Less involvement

from **Boards That Make a Difference**, *Carver J, (Jossey-Bass, 1990)*

The degree of involvement did not seem to matter, surprisingly. Involvement, in itself, and when isolated from a more comprehensive approach to rectifying flaws, was not the answer. Neither was the adoption of a particular dominant style, whereby the governing body saw itself and behaved mainly as (I paraphrase):

- watch dog, keeping a wary eye on staff
- cheerleader, offering unconditional support
- manager, trying to run the school
- planner, planning everything in detail
- communicator, acting as a public relations unit

adapted from **Boards That Make a Difference**, *Carver J, (Jossey-Bass, 1990)*

Of course, some aspects of these approaches are appropriate in certain circumstances, but no one prescription is valid in isolation. It is worth remembering the five roles of governing bodies (see Appendix I, page 81) identified in **"Lessons In Teamwork"** (Audit Commission and Ofsted, 1995):

Steering
Monitoring
Executive
Accountability
Support

from **Lessons In Teamwork: How School Governing Bodies Can Become More Effective**, *(Audit Commission/Ofsted, 1995)*

The point here is that each role is as important as any other. Any one governor might be involved in one or more of these roles at any one time. During his or her term of office, he or she will have been involved in all five roles at one time or another.

In **"Boards That Make a Difference"**, Carver argues that a more complete and dynamic approach be taken by a governing body wishing to improve its effectiveness. Whilst this approach is addressed to the governing body as a whole, it provides a helpful context for the individual governor to identify his or her priorities and foci. Carver suggests fourteen steps or actions that could lead to "a new governance":

- Cradle the vision
- Explicitly address fundamental values
- Force an external focus
- Force forward thinking
- Separate large issues from small
- Enable proactivity
- Enable an outcome-driven organising system
- Facilitate diversity and unity
- Describe relationships to relevant constituencies
- Define a common basis for discipline
- Delineate the governing body's role in common topics
- Determine what information is needed
- Balance overcontrol and undercontrol
- Use governing body time efficiently

(from **Boards That Make a Difference**; *Carver, J., (Jossey-Bass, 1990)*

Task 14
A New
Governance

Following my commentary on each of Carver's points, assess yourself and your governing body against each point. (This is a long task. You will find it more manageable if you attempt it in "bite-sized chunks", rather than as one long study task.)

● **Cradle the vision**

The governing body needs to develop and nurture its vision of the school and itself in the future, returning to it regularly. The vision should underpin everything the governing body does.

> **Questions**
>
> What is my vision?
> What is our vision?
> How far does it form the basis of all I/we do?
> How frequently do I/we refer to it in our decision and policy making?

● **Explicitly address fundamental values**

Being clear about and agreeing the shared values of the governing body is essential. As we saw in *Task 1* (page 14) our values often lie deep within us and remain unspoken, but affect our views and decisions in fundamental ways. Getting them out in the open and seeing clearly where they are shared or are in conflict, is vital to the coherence of the governing body.

> **Questions**
>
> What are our collective values?
> Have we discussed them?
> Are they written down and/or published anywhere?
> How would a new governor joining the team know what our values are?
> To what extent are my values compatible with those of the governing body?

- **Force an external focus**
- **Force forward thinking**
- **Separate large issues from small**
- **Enable proactivity**

Governing bodies are often too inward looking and need to focus on the wider and future context of the school, seeing the bigger picture. This will help to avoid concentration on trivia. Becoming proactive is a likely outcome of a systematic and regular anticipation of what the future holds.

One way of achieving this is to carry out a simple PESTLE analysis. As individuals, in groups or as a whole group, list the foreseeable developments in these areas:

political	e.g. local election; general election - various parties' policies
economic	e.g. Local Education Authority retention of a larger proportion of educational budget; 100% delegation to schools of the remainder
social	e.g. growth in the number of working mothers and more fathers at home
technological	e.g. cable modems; TV, computer, telephone and fax in one box
legislative	e.g. Green Paper on Special Educational Needs
environmental	e.g. projected growth or decline of your local community; road building projects

Then consider how they might impact on the school and what the school might need to do in order to anticipate the impact.

For example, in relation to social change, you might need to consider offering a breakfast facility to pupils. A cost-benefit analysis would help to identify the relative merits of such a proposal.

Questions

How far ahead do I/we look when discussing the development of the school:
one year? two years? five? ten?
Have/we carried out a PESTLE analysis?
What have we learned from the analysis?
How will I/we be affected by the White Paper **"Excellence In Schools?"**
What sort of topics, issues and subjects do I/we spend my/our time on?

● **Enable an outcome-driven organising system**

For some, the processes involved in education are more important than the products. It matters more to those who hold this view that pupils enjoy learning and benefit from all sorts of unexpected and unplanned spin-offs, than that they all achieve a particular examination result or qualification at the end.

For others, the product is what matters most. For them, the end (an examination result, say) justifies the means, to a large extent. This is, of course, to polarise the debate and in reality, process and product are, arguably, equally important. John Carver believes that a focus on the end-product or outcome should be the driving force for the way the governing body works. For him, governing bodies should be very clear about their goals and targets over time, and should organise themselves so as to ensure that the outcomes are achieved.

The renewed national focus on targets and target-setting will encourage this to happen, in relation to Heads, teachers and governing bodies. **"Excellence In Schools"** states:

Setting school targets

> From September 1988, each school will be required to have challenging targets for improvement. If schools are to take their targets seriously, it is important that they should take direct responsibility for them. Governing bodies as part of their strategic role...should take time to consider all the available information and discuss in detail their school's targets, together with proposals from the headteacher on the necessary improvement plans to achieve them.
>
> School targets should be based on:
>
> ● benchmark (i.e. comparative) information on the performance of similar schools, at national and local level;
>
> ● information on the rate of progress needed to achieve national targets;
>
> ● the most recent inspection evidence.
>
> *from* **Excellence In Schools**, *DfEE (The Stationery Office Ltd, 1997, Crown Copyright)*

It's worth emphasising, however, that targets are most easily set in relation to academic achievement. Whilst this is one of the central foci of the school, there are many equally important outcomes to be achieved, such as improving pupils'- especially boys'- attitudes to learning, and in these areas it is harder, though not impossible, to set targets.

Targets need to be SMART to be effective. That is

Specific
Measurable
Achievable
Realistic
Time-constrained.

The *School Development Plan* is the key document in which to express those targets. Well-designed targets make the job of monitoring and evaluation considerably more manageable for governors and teachers alike.

Questions

Have I/we undertaken any training on target setting?
What information do I/we gather to help us know how the school is doing?
(e.g. SATs data; GCSE results.)
What else do I/we need to know?
(e.g. pupils' previous performance; staffing changes during recent years.)
From where am I/are we going to get it?
(e.g. Headteacher; relevant school documents.)

● **Facilitate diversity and unity:**

These two are not as incompatible as they may seem at first sight. The membership of the governing body is bound to be - indeed, is intended to be - diverse, in that it should contain people from all walks of life, with varied backgrounds and experience. That diversity is an essential component of the governing body:

> People who are similar in their attitudes, values and beliefs tend to form stable enduring groups. Homogeneity tends in general to promote satisfaction. Heterogeneous groups tend to exhibit more conflict, but most studies show them to be more productive than the homogenous groups.
>
> *from* **Understanding Organizations**, *Handy C, (Penguin Books, 1993)*

So a governing body should exploit its diversity, maximise the collective talents of all its members, welcome healthy friction between colleagues working towards the solution of a problem and take full advantage of fluctuations in membership. This is easier said than done, since we human beings tend towards stability and security rather than change and risk.

At the same time, the governing body needs always to work towards consensus on all important issues, achieving good decisions from thoughtful debate and discussion. The notion of collective responsibility is vital: *whatever your view of a decision, once made it must be supported.*

Questions

How diverse is my governing body?
How far do I observe the principle of collective responsibility?
How far do others do observe the principle of collective responsibility?

- **Describe relationships to relevant constituencies**

This is a delicate subject and one which can cause confusion. It helps to remember that governors are representatives, in some cases, of the groups who elected them, *but not their delegates*. In other words, for example, the teacher governor is there to represent the general view of the teaching staff as a whole, rather than the views of a smaller group of like-minded teachers.

This is particularly important when matters come to a vote. Each governor must make up his or her own mind about the proposal and vote according to his or her conscience, having listened carefully to and considered all aspects of the debate. No governor should unthinkingly follow a "party line". It is important for all sides - teachers; governors; Head and Deputy(ies); parents and children; the wider community - to be clear about the role of the governing body in relation to each set of "stakeholders". This should avoid misunderstandings in the future. To quote from **"Guidance on Good Governance"**:

Governors are elected or appointed by different groups - including parents, teachers and others within the local community. By these means, although they are not delegates, the governing body reflects the community it serves.

from **Guidance on Good Governance**, *DfEE (The Stationery Office Ltd.,1996 Crown Copyright)*

Questions

Do I see myself as a representative or delegate?
Who or what is my constituency?
How do I ensure that I reflect the genuine views of others?

- **Define a common basis for discipline**

A governing body might agree to sign up collectively to a common Code of Conduct, which would govern their behaviour and proceedings in a general sense, expressing the spirit of good governance. Indeed, the DfEE's **"Guidance on Good Governance"** is an excellent document which could serve this purpose, if the governing body so chose. The Guidance includes the seven principles of public life drawn up by the Nolan Committee. These provide a firm moral framework in which the governing body should operate:

Selflessness

Holders of public office should take decisions solely in terms of the public interest. They should not do so in order to gain financial or other material benefits for themselves, their family or their friends.

Integrity

Holders of public office should not place themselves under any financial or other obligation to outside individuals or organisations that might influence them in the performance of their official duties.

Objectivity

In carrying out public business, including making public appointments, awarding contracts, or recommending individuals for rewards and benefits, holders of public office should make choices on merit.

Accountability

Holders of public office are accountable for their decisions and actions to the public and must submit themselves to whatever scrutiny is appropriate to their office.

Openness

Holders of public office should be as open as possible about all the decisions and actions that they take. They should give reasons for their decisions and restrict information only when the wider public interest clearly demands this.

Honesty

Holders of public office have a duty to declare any private interests relating to their public duties and to take steps to resolve any conflicts arising in a way that protects the public interest.

Leadership

Holders of public office should promote and support these principles by leadership and example.

From **Second Report of the Committee on Standards in Public Life** (CM3270 May, 1996, Crown Copyright)

It might be a useful exercise to compare your list of values which you drew up in *Section One*, page (14), with this list of principles.

The governing body might also consider agreeing to a set of Standing Orders, which cover the detailed processes of governance, including legal matters. Sample and model policies are available from a variety of sources, including Local Education Authority Governor Support teams and Headteachers' professional associations. Any governing body considering this should also to refer to its *Instruments and Articles of Government* and **"School Governors: a Guide to the Law"** (DfEE, June 1997 Crown Copyright).

> **Questions**
>
> What disciplinary or moral framework do I observe as a governor?
>
> What are the implications of the seven principles of public life for my standards and behaviour as a member of a governing body? (e.g. have I registered any pecuniary interests I might have?)
>
> In what ways can it be demonstrated that my governing body lives up to the seven principles? (e.g. we publish the draft minutes of our meetings as soon as possible; we open our meetings to a variety of contributors and observers.)

● **Delineate the governing body's role in common topics**

An effective governing body will have agreed a *Scheme of Delegation* that determines and defines the various responsibilities of the Head and the governing body. Governing bodies have the power to delegate some, but not all, of their responsibilities to the Head and this needs to be negotiated and written down. The *Scheme of Delegation* should also include the terms of reference for its committees.

Questions

What are the terms of reference for the committees on which I serve?
How clear am I about my role in, for example, curriculum matters?

● **Determine what information is needed**

This is easier said than done, in some cases. There is more need than ever for the governing body to have access to good quality, selected information, especially in relation to pupil progress and achievement overall. The Head will be the main provider of this information, but needs to know what the governing body wants.

However, do you know what you want? Do you know what is - or could be made - available? There is a need for discussion and negotiation here. Governors often complain of being over-loaded with paperwork. Whilst information is power, it only works if you limit what you receive to the kind of things you really want and need to know.

Questions

What information do I need? (e.g. monthly budget information in an understandable form.)
What information do I get? (e.g. computerised budget print-outs that I don't understand.)
What else do I need to know? (e.g. where does the school's budget come from?)
How am I going to get it? (e.g. ask the Chair of the Finance Committee; attend an appropriate training course.)

● **Balance overcontrol and undercontrol**

You may have heard of the idea of "tight - loose" organisational structures. The idea is based on the fact that in any one person's area of work or responsibility, there must be some "no go" areas, where essential rules must be obeyed without question, such as fire regulations, for example. A similar sort of restriction might apply to the vision statement, where, once negotiated and agreed, all work towards it. On the other hand, there should be some aspects of the work or responsibility where you have more autonomy to decide how and when to do something. The governing body needs a clear and respected framework within which the creativity of each member can be free to operate effectively.

- **Use governing body time efficiently**

Governing bodies meet as a whole five or six times a year, as we have seen. That time is precious to the individuals and the group. It makes sense to use the time available to maximum advantage. An effective Chair and Clerk; timed agendas with clearly stated purposes for each item; pre-reading carried out by all governors; a focus on the items which really matter - all of these things (and more) can maximise the use of the time available. The same applies to committee meetings, of course.

To sum up, you have considered the implications of John Carver's proposals for "a new governance":

- Cradle the vision
- Explicitly address fundamental values
- Force an external focus
- Force forward thinking
- Separate large issues from small
- Enable proactivity
- Enable an outcome-driven organising system
- Facilitate diversity and unity
- Describe relationships to relevant constituencies
- Define a common basis for discipline
- Delineate the governing body's role in common topics
- Determine what information is needed
- Balance overcontrol and undercontrol
- Use governing body time efficiently

from **Boards That Make a Difference**, *Carver J., (Jossey-Bass, 1990)*

What you have learned will depend upon your starting point and degree of familiarity with the work of governing bodies and the nature of the governing body of which you are a member. I hope that you will have found a good degree of correlation between your values, objectives and attitudes and the approaches to good governance advocated by John Carver. I hope, too, that it will have given you some useful questions to ask of your governing body now and in the future.

However, reality seldom matches our ideals. The kind of governance we have been considering is possible to achieve, but all governing bodies are different - and some are more effective than others. One of the key tasks facing any governor is to identify and understand what makes a group effective and how, as an individual, he or she can contribute to the improvement of the group's effectiveness. It is to this that we will now turn our attention.

2   Roles in the Team

Whether we do so consciously or subconsciously, we always play a role of some kind when we are in a group. It may be a role we create for ourselves, or one which is thrust upon us. In a governing body, members may play many different roles at different times. Observing and understanding the roles of others in the group can help us to identify the role we play, or would like to play in the future. Much of this depends upon common sense gained through experience and we all have some experience of being a member of a group, whether it be a family, sports team, work group or whatever. There has been much research carried out in relation to this subject and it can provide some useful pointers to our own development and understanding.

The roles people play in a group/team were identified, memorably, by R M Belbin in **"Management Teams-Why They Succeed or Fail"**, (Heinemann; 1981). Following extended research, he suggested that the following roles are needed for a fully effective group. *(NB. He emphasises that "he" means humankind and refers to both genders.)*

The Chairman

He is the one who presides over the team and co-ordinates its efforts. He need be in no sense brilliant or creative, but would rather be called disciplined, focused and balanced. He talks and listens well, is a good judge of people and of things; a man who works through others.

The Shaper

The Shaper is highly-strung, outgoing and dominant. He is the task leader and in the absence of the Chairman would leap into that role, even though he might not do it any too well. His strength lies in his drive and in his passion for the task, but he can be over-sensitive, irritable and impatient. He is needed as the spur to action.

The Plant

Unlike the Shaper, the Plant is introverted but is intellectually dominant. He is the source of original ideas and proposals, being the most imaginative as well as the most intelligent member of the team. He can, however, be careless of details and may resent criticism. He needs to be drawn out or he will switch off.

The Monitor-Evaluator

The Monitor-Evaluator is also intelligent, but it is an analytical rather than a creative intelligence. His contribution is the careful dissection of ideas and the ability to see the flaw in an argument. He is often less involved than the others, tucked away with his data, aloof from the team, but necessary as a quality check. He is dependable but can be tactless and cold.

The Resource-Investigator

This is the most popular member of the team, extrovert, sociable and relaxed. He it is who brings new contacts, ideas and developments to the group, the salesman, diplomat or liaison officer. He is not himself original or a driver, and therefore needs the team to pick up his contributions.

The Company Worker

The Company Worker is the practical organiser. He it is who turns ideas into manageable tasks. Schedules, charts and plans are his thing. Methodical, trustworthy and efficient, he is not excited by visions and can be unexciting himself. He does not lead but is adept at administering.

The Team Worker

The Team Worker holds the team together in another way, by being supportive to others, by listening, encouraging, harmonising and understanding. Likeable and popular but uncompetitive, he is the sort of person you do not notice when he's there but miss when he isn't.

The Finisher

Without the Finisher the team might never meet its deadlines. He it is who checks the details, worries about schedules and chivvies the others with his sense of urgency. His relentless follow-through is important but not always popular.

from **Management Teams: Why They Succeed or Fail**, *Belbin R M,*
(Butterworth-Heinemann, 1981)

How applicable are these roles to the effective governing body? I would say - very! The role of the Chair, for instance, is absolutely critical to the efficiency and openness of the group. It is in some ways an unenviable position and calls for a wide range of skills and qualities, such as patience, perseverance, time management, a sense of fairness and so on. In a governing body, the Chair has no powers in addition to those of the group as a whole, but is usually the person who has most direct and regular contact with the head. Managing to be both the equal of all other governors, and at the same time the focal point of the governing body, is a very difficult act to pull off.

Does it matter if any one of these "characters" is missing from the team? What if we've got more than one of one type? Belbin's answer is:

 Too many of one type in a team means a lack of balance; too few roles and some tasks do not get done. In a small team, therefore, one person may have to perform more than one role...more stable groups get by without the full set of roles.

from **Management Teams: Why They Succeed or Fail,** *Belbin R M,*
(Butterworth-Heinemann, 1981)

So there is room for flexibility and manoeuvre - but if all your fellow governors are "Shapers", for example, you've got problems! When vacancies occur on the governing body, some careful reassessment of what the group needs in terms of "role-players" is well worth carrying out. Achieving a balance of roles is hard enough: maintaining the balance as governors come and go is even harder.

My guess is that, as you were reading these descriptions, you were assessing both yourself and your fellow governors against them. If I am right, the next task should be fairly straightforward

3   Finding Your Role

Having considered the importance of roles - and the range of roles required by a governing body - you might now consider the role you most commonly play in your governing body. Weigh up your fellow governors and write their names against whichever role they play most frequently.

Task 15
Finding Your
Role

Role	Me	Fellow Governors
Chairman		
Shaper		
Plant		
Monitor-evaluator		
Resource investigator		
Company worker		
Team worker		
Finisher		

When you have completed the table as fully as you can, consider whether there are any gaps? Does it matter if there are? How balanced is the group overall? How and where do you fit in? Are you playing the right role(s), the one(s) that suit you best, or have you been forced by circumstances to play a role with which you are uncomfortable? If so, what could you do to change this? Could you, or any of your colleagues, develop in such a way as to fill the gaps that you may have identified?

An analysis such as this is not particularly "scientific", but it can help to identify strengths and weaknesses in the team and act as a useful spur to improvement, both at a personal and group level. There may be, for example, an opportunity here for you to seek some personal or professional development. Alternatively, this could provide a useful way of identifying the best new recruit to the governing body.

Having clarified your actual and potential role(s) in the group, let us now consider how you can contribute effectively in meetings of the governing body and its committees.

4   Effectiveness in Meetings

A governing body meets as a whole group maybe five or six times a year. It will usually establish a series of committees (not sub-committees, incidentally, since the governing body is not in itself a committee, so there can be no *sub-committees*) which will meet at different times and with variable frequency. A Finance Committee is likely to meet monthly, for example, whereas a Premises Committee may meet once a term. The organisation will be described in the governing body's *Scheme of Delegation*.

So the full governing body meeting is crucial. It is the arena or the forum in which you will be seen by *all* your colleagues. It is here that decisions are made. It is here that you can make an impact. The way it runs is vital to the overall success or failure of the governing body as a whole.

An effective meeting is well organised, allowing a free discussion of agenda items where every member of the governing body is encouraged to make a contribution. Decisions, and actions arising from decisions, should be clearly understood by all those present.

The meeting is unlikely to be fully successful unless some or all of the following conditions are met:

- The agenda and papers for the meeting have been received and understood beforehand.
- The room layout is conducive to comfort and concentration, including attention to heating, ventilation and light.
- The proceedings are chaired well and keep to time.
- Attendance is good.
- Everybody present understands and observes the ground rules of meetings.

If you have little or no experience of group meetings, the proceedings may seem arcane and unduly formal. As I have stressed before, a very important part of your induction should be designed to help you make sense of the first and subsequent meetings. There are, undoubtedly, people who thrive on the finer procedural points of meetings but the level of formality should be decided by the governing body together.

Even if the meeting is fairly informal, it can still seem daunting to make your first contribution to the discussion. You don't necessarily need to make a major impact from the word go, but the longer you leave it, the harder it is to ask a question or make a comment. Here are some tips about how to make an early contribution:

- Read all the papers for the meeting beforehand. Check your understanding with a fellow governor and prepare a question on one or more of the topics covered.

- Ask the Chair for clarification of something you're not quite sure about. Don't be afraid to do this - no-one can expect you to understand everything from the start.

- Volunteer for a task you know you can tackle successfully, if volunteers are sought.

- Offer to review or write an induction policy, ideally with another governor. However, don't imply a major criticism of the governing body in doing so.

Bear in mind that the quality, frequency, subject matter and tone of your first few contributions will create an impression in the minds of your colleagues about who you are and your role in the group. First impressions count and other people's perceptions of you set hard quite quickly. Beware of creating an image of yourself that is untrue to your values and which limits the way you operate in the future.

Having made some contributions to discussions, and begun to establish yourself within the group, you could think about some or all of the following questions. (We will look at each set of questions in turn, in *Tasks 16, 19* and *20*.)

Q

Who am I in this group?
What are others' expectations of me?
Am I here to listen or to lead?
Am I a representative or present in my own right?
Who is judging me on my performance?

Who has power in the group?
What kind of power is it?
Do I want to change the pattern of influence?
If so, how do I do it?

Are my goals in line with those of the group?
Should they be?
What should I do about them if they are not?
If one of my needs is to be liked and accepted, how important is that for me?

from **Understanding Organizations,** *Handy C, (Penguin Books, 1993)*

Much of this book has been designed to make and keep you aware of these sorts of issues and your feelings about them. Developing and acting upon this awareness will enable you to be a more effective member of the governing body.

It is all too easy to fall into a particular role and then find it very hard to break out of it. Groups tend to produce conformity and it can be hard to challenge ideas and decisions which threaten that conformity. We've seen that there are common key roles necessary in a fully effective team. That doesn't mean that any one person may only ever play one particular role. Doing so leads to stagnation of ideas and lack of flexibility. In addition to Belbin's role definitions, Handy suggests that there are other common archetypes, such as:

The comedian

He or she is valuable in relaxing tension, in providing a willing butt for other members of the group and in particular the chairman. When, however, the task becomes dominant the comedian is often discarded as being no longer necessary. People who are insecure often can find this role a quick way of establishing an identity within a group. It brings popularity - is threatening to no-one. Unfortunately, the comedian's role is a hard one to escape from. Many people are overlooked in groups because they initially seized on this role.

The organiser

Usually taken by an extrovert character at the outset when the group is relieved that any leader should emerge. He or she establishes their identity within the group by becoming their spokesperson or leader on anything that does not call for the presence or action of the formal leader. Physical arrangements, social activities and a lot of chore-like jobs come his or her way and are willingly taken on.

The commentator

Not a popular role since it involves some threat to the other members. The occupant, often clever but disillusioned, takes it upon him - or herself to maintain an occasional commentary on the proceedings, e.g. "By my reckoning we have now spent one hour discussing the opening paragraph of the report..." This activity is often useful but is seldom seen to be so by the other group members.

The deviant

One way to establish one's identity is to exploit any differences that there may be between you and the group. For instance, a reputation for always asking for definitions can be exploited, sometimes humorously, to give someone an early role in a group. Others make a role out of always opposing anything. To become a common enemy is a sure way of attracting attention. Members of minority groups often use this fact to gain the role of legitimate deviant.

from **Understanding Organizations,** *Handy C, (Penguin Books, 1993)*

No doubt you could add to this list from your own experience. You might play the game of analysing your fellow governors according to these and other role definitions. What matters, however, is to identify and recognise the roles that you wish to play and see how far they correspond to the roles you actually play.

Whether you are there to listen or to lead is up to you. You must decide how active and assertive you wish to be. Remember that all governors are equal:

> The governing body are a group. Individual governors have no power except where the whole governing body have delegated a specific power to that individual.
>
> *from* **School Governors: A Guide to the Law**, *DfEE, (The Stationery Office Ltd., 1997, Crown Copyright)*

Responsibility is collective. During the DfEE/Ofsted Governors' Conference in March 1996, Joan Sallis emphasised the need for governors to accept responsibility for the work of the governing body:

> It was easy to say: "Somebody elected that idiot to the Chair again while I was looking for my glasses", or "That chair and the vice-chair and a mate of theirs then decided they were going to choose the new deputy head...Now, Joan, you've told us that's illegal; it's illegal if we don't elect them. Will you come and tell them it's illegal because they won't believe me?" Or: "Who put all that junk on the agenda? We never got round to discuss the important things at all."
>
> But these things had happened because governors had let them happen.
>
> *from* **Teamwork for School Improvement: A Report of the DfEE/Ofsted Governors' Conference** *DfEE (The Stationery Office Ltd., 1996, Crown Copyright)*

What you can do, and arguably should do, is seek to influence the group as a whole in its decision making and other activities. We will look at how you might do this later on. Just listening is not an option, although one or two "passengers" still behave like this. You don't need to be the Chair in order to lead. It may be that you choose to take a lead in carrying out some research on behalf of the governing body or, perhaps co-ordinating an event or publication. On other occasions you may be content to listen and then contribute to a discussion.

> However, it's very important that the governing body does not become divided into an "A" and "B" team, where "As" do all the hard work and leadership and the "Bs" merely listen and do nothing.
>
> The strength of the governing body lies in the talents of its members, and in their ability to work together as a team. Each governor has an equal right to participate and to state his or her view, while respecting the views of others.
>
> Each governor makes up his or her own mind about issues that are considered by governing bodies. Once decisions are made by the group, individual governors are bound by them and should be loyal to them.
>
> *from* **Guidance on Good Governance**, *DfEE (The Stationery Office Ltd., 1996 Crown Copyright)*

We have clarified the fact that, if you are an elected governor, you are a representative of that electorate as a whole rather than its delegate. You are also there in your own right. This can be very problematic, especially if you are a parent governor in a large school. How can you know what the majority of parents feel about any issue? Of course, there are other parent governors on the governing body so you might choose to establish a common understanding with them. You might also consider regular surveys of parental opinion. The parents' questionnaire included in the **"Ofsted Inspection Resource Pack"** is a good example of a simple format that can be very informative. It asks parents to indicate the extent to which they agree or disagree with statements like:

I feel the school encourages parents to play an active part in the life of the school

The school handles complaints from parents well

The school achieves high standards of good behaviour

from **The Ofsted Handbook: Inspection Resource Pack**, *Ofsted (HMSO 1995, Crown Copyright)*

Schools may also add to these questions. Appointed governors are there in their own right, by and large. It varies from one Local Education Authority to another, but Local Education Authority governors tend not to pursue a party political line. The idea underpinning the composition of a governing body is one of representation in miniature of the community served by the school.

You are being judged on your performance by fellow governors, the headteacher and staff, your electorate and yourself. You must decide for yourself how far you are willing to live up to other people's expectations of you, assuming you can ever know what they may be. If your electorate disapproves of the way you behave, they can choose not to re-elect you if you are still eligible and want to stand for election after your first term of office expires.

Most important is to evaluate yourself. We tend to be our own harshest self-critics, so we should have little to fear from colleagues' opinions. Find a sympathetic fellow governor and ask him/her what he/she thinks of the way you operate, if you want a second opinion.

Task 16
Who Am I in this Group?

Answer these questions

Who am I in this group?

What are others' expectations of me?

Am I here to listen or to lead?

Am I a representative or present in my own right?

Who is judging me on my performance?

Task 17

Judging Your
Behaviour

Ask yourself whether, and in what circumstances, you have ever helped to block the group's progress by any of the following strategies:

Restricting information: you knew the answer but you didn't tell.

Lying: you deliberately distorted the facts in order to preserve a position in the group.

Pairing: you broke into a sub-group rather than trying to solve the problem together.

Fighting: you engaged in a win-lose conflict within the group.

Flight: you withdrew, by, for example leaving the room (physically or psychologically), sulking, sleeping, doodling, telephoning.

Noise: you spoke to be heard rather than to contribute.

Suppressing emotion: you demanded logic and rationality when emotions were part of the problem or the solution.

(adapted from **Managing People at Work***, Hunt J, (McGraw-Hill, 1992)*

It takes a certain amount of brutal honesty to admit these sorts of behaviours but most of us do things like this from time to time, however noble we like to think we are!

It's also important to work out why you may have adopted these behaviours.

What were the circumstances?
What were you trying to achieve?
Was it successful?
Did the end justify the means?
How did you feel about your behaviour at the time?
How do you feel about it now?
What did your colleagues feel about it?
Can you see yourself acting like this again, at a future meeting?
What do you feel about other people who act as you did?

This kind of self-reflection can help you to be more aware of your behaviour, and that of others, and ensure that your future behaviour contributes to the positive development of the group.

Most of the behaviours described above are verbal and, as such, can be easier to spot and understand. All verbal behaviour is, of course, accompanied by non-verbal behaviour, which can complement the explicit communication or confuse or even contradict it. Sometimes we react badly to somebody not because of what they said but because of the expression on their face as they said it. An aggressive posture can mean that our reasonable argument is interpreted as a criticism by one or more of our colleagues. *Task 18* is designed to help you recognise and interpret certain combinations of non-verbal communication.

Like our fellow mammals, we all give out signals to others who interpret them, often subconsciously. Similarly, we interpret the non-verbal behaviour of our colleagues, whether we actively choose to do so or not. Whilst there are no certain right answers to our interpretations, the majority of people interpret "clusters" of such signals in common ways. Look through the following clusters and note how you would interpret them in each case. (The answers are at the foot of the page.)

1

Don't look at the other person
Avoid eye contact and immediately
look away when it happens
Clench your hands
Cross your arms
Constantly rub an eye, nose or ear
Lean away from the other person
Cross your legs
Swivel your feet towards the door

2

Blink your eyes frequently
Lick your lips
Keep clearing your throat
Open and close your hands frequently
Put your hand over your mouth while
speaking
Tug at an ear
Fidget in your chair
Jig your feet up and down

3

Stare at the other person
Have a wry "I've heard it all before"
type of smile
Raise your eyebrows in exaggerated
amazement or disbelief
Look over the top of your spectacles
Point your finger at the other person
Thump your fist on the table
Rub the back of your neck
Stand while the other person remains seated
Stride around
If seated, lean right back with both hands
behind your head and your legs spread out
in front of you

4

Look at the other person's face
Smile
Nod your head as the other person
is talking
Have open hands
Hand to face occasionally
Uncrossed arms and legs
Lean forward slightly
Move closer to the other person

5

Look into the other person's eyes
Don't blink your eyes
Thrust your chin forward
Keep hands away from your face
"Steeple" your finger tips together
If standing, have hands together behind
you in an "at ease" position
If seated, lean back with legs out in front
of you
If standing, keep straight
Stay still, no sudden movements, no
wriggling

6

When listening, look at the other person
for about 3/4 of the time
Tilt your head to one side slightly
Hand to cheek
Slowly stroke your chin or pinch the
bridge of your nose
If you wear spectacles, take them off and
put an earframe in your mouth
Lean forward to speak
Lean back to listen
Keep your legs still

adapted from **Face To Face Skills**, *Honey P, (Gower, 1988)*

1 defensive   2 anxious   3 overbearing and aggressive   4 friendly and co-operative   5 confident   6 thoughtful

It is not my intention here to make you acutely self-conscious about your non-verbal behaviour, nor to suggest that you consciously attempt to analyse every aspect of colleagues' tics, twitches, smiles and shrugs. Nevertheless, being aware of your own signals and how they might be interpreted can help you to counter unintended "messages" being transmitted. It can also make you more wary of over-interpreting the way others look and behave.

Inevitably, groups contain a mixture of people with varying degrees of influence over the group as a whole. Although all governors are equal, some always have an influence on decisions, some do some of the time and some seldom - or even never. This may or may not be to do with their position in the group (e.g. Chair or Vice Chair) or school (e.g. headteacher). Their influence may be benign or malign, depending on a host of factors, including basic personal values, understanding the purpose and responsibilities of their role and so forth. We looked at sources of personal authority in *Section One*. Remember that power derives from any one or more of:

- ☛ Your role in the group
- ☛ Your expertise or knowledge
- ☛ Your charisma or personal authority
- ☛ Your control of resources

By now, you will know the source of your potential or real power to influence the group. Through a repertoire of strategies and behaviours, as we have seen, you can ensure that your contribution to the group's effectiveness is both benign and significant. You do not need to accept the *status quo*, nor feel incapable of exerting influence on the group as a whole. *Task 19* looks more closely at this.

In addition to having analysed your own source of personal authority, you need to do the same in relation to your colleagues in order to understand their influence on the group as a whole. Complete this table:

Task 19
Who Has Power in the Group?

Answer these questions

Who has power in the group?
What kind of power is it?
Do I want to change the pattern of influence?
If so, how do I do it?

Who has power and what sort of power is it?

Governor	Source of Personal Authority or Power

How do you go about exerting your own influence?

I made some initial suggestions earlier on in this Section. Let's pursue it a little further. In **"Understanding Organisations"**, Charles Handy identifies a variety of methods of influence based on these sources of power. In summary, he writes about:

> **Force** the crudest method of influence, it derives from physical or, sometimes, resource power. In a team or between individuals, it is usually expressed as bullying behaviour
>
> **Rules/ procedures** which work as long as the person making them has the perceived right to institute them and the means and the will to enforce them. They derive from position power, backed by resource power.
>
> **Exchange bargaining; negotiating; cajoling.** They can derive from any source of power but usually derive from resource and position power.
>
> **Persuasion** relying on logic, the power of argument and the evidence of the facts. It usually gets contaminated by one or more of the other methods. Expertise or personal power are the likeliest sources.
>
> **Ecology** sets the conditions for behaviour. Inattention to the environment of your meetings, for example, can make things difficult, if not impossible. It is larger than the environmental issues, too, encompassing the size of the group, the time available, the decision-making method and so on.
>
> **Magnetism** the application of personal power or charisma. It can show itself as trust, respect, charm or infectious enthusiasm, but is almost impossible to define.
>
> *from* **Understanding Organizations,** *Handy C, (Penguin Books, 1993)*

Being aware of the possible uses of your power and influence can help you to select the appropriate approach to achieving your ends in any given situation.

Let's look at some specific issues.

Do you know how to get an item onto the governing body meeting agenda?
Is there a set procedure?
Who writes the agenda, anyway?

It should be the work of the Chair and Clerk, primarily. They should encourage and ensure contributions from any governing body colleague. Where this doesn't happen, the Chair is likely to exercise undue power and influence over the governing body and it becomes progressively less open and democratic. This is usually by default rather than design. It is up to you to ensure that your issues are raised and discussed.

Having secured a place on the agenda for your item, you need also to think through how best to present it. Often a supporting paper, sent out in advance of the meeting, is a useful strategy. This can highlight the main points you wish to get across. Of course, you cannot guarantee that all your colleagues will read it before the meeting, but some will and that's part of the job done before the meeting even begins. It's up to the Chair to introduce your item and then the floor's yours.

 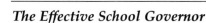

You may not be the world's greatest public speaker but you don't have to be. Speaking in public like this can be daunting, so it's worth rehearsing what you want to say. For example, talk to yourself in the car. The only people who might be disturbed by this are any passengers - or occupants of other vehicles at a set of traffic lights! Persuade a friend or family member to listen to your presentation. It's not cheating to do this and the only danger is that the presentation becomes stale and artificial, so don't overdo it.

I realise that I might be making it seem like a "bigger deal" than it actually is, so, again, don't go overboard. Make sure that you get your main points across succinctly and clearly. If you are offering alternatives or making a proposal, make sure the options are very clearly laid out. If you want to be reasonably sure of success, try to get one or two other governors on your side before the meeting. However, you need to tread carefully here to avoid any suggestion of a covert group being set up, or an unofficial governing body meeting taking place outside of the main meeting. I'm simply suggesting a chat with a couple of colleagues on the phone or at the school gate to see what sort of a reaction you can expect and what level of support you are likely to get.

Changing patterns of influence is extremely difficult and demanding. It may be that everything is fine and no individual or small group unduly influences the whole group. My experience suggests that this is not always the case, however. Undue influence can arise as a result of any number of circumstances, including the following scenarios:

- Chairs of governing bodies can easily become over-dominant, often without realising it, especially if the other governors rely on the Chair to do most of the hard work, as does happen.

- Because the Chair and headteacher have to work together closely, their joint power can be formidable and they can sometimes present a governing body with a series of *faits accompli*, having decided in advance what should be the "right" decision.

- Some "rogue" governors can intimidate colleagues by behaving aggressively; challenging every decision indiscriminately and failing to observe common courtesies and the ground rules.

- Where factionalism reflects the two or more sides of local politics (with a small "p"), as I've said before, the consequences can be disastrous.

There are plenty of other examples; I am sure you could add some from your own experience. In such circumstances it is yet more important for the governing body to exert its collective power and peer-group pressure. Sadly, because governors are volunteers and have many concerns other than the tensions in the governing body, after struggling with such difficulties for a while, they may be tempted to "throw in the towel" rather than work together towards a solution.

So what can you do, as an individual? A new governor often finds it hard to "break in" to an established group. It can help if you are not alone. If you are lucky there will be other new governors joining at the same time as you, or if not, soon after you join. These people are, in some ways, your natural allies, although you may subsequently discover that you have more in common with a different colleague or two. It's worth exploring with other new colleagues where the common ground may lie.

There are subtle ways of influencing other people's behaviour. In **"Face to Face Skills"**, Peter Honey offers some helpful strategies based on observation and experiment. He suggests, for example, that you "flag" your behaviour frequently to avoid misinterpretation of your motives and aims. He identifies some common phrases that people use to "flag" their intentions:

Suggesting

"This is an idea off the top of my head..."
"I'd like to put up an Aunt Sally for you to kick around..."

Proposing

"I propose that..."

Building

"I've just been thinking about Bill's earlier idea that we...I'd like to add to it by suggesting..."
"I like that idea! Can I develop it further by proposing..."

Supporting

"I'd like to say something in support of that..."

Stating difficulties

"I'd like to play devil's advocate with that idea for a few minutes..."

Disagreeing

"I'm going to disagree with that and explain why..."

Seeking clarification

"Could I just check that I have got this straight? As I understand it you are suggesting that..."

from **Face To Face Skills**, *Honey P, (Gower, 1988)*

There are many examples of such "flagging" statements and it's useful to develop a repertoire which can be drawn upon when appropriate. Honey goes on to offer the following advice about getting the response you want from one or more colleagues:

If you want the other person to propose (i.e. state, announce, instruct a possible course of action), ask them for ideas.

If you want the other person to suggest (i.e. express a possible course of action as a question), ask for ideas or support what they were saying.

If you want the other person to build on an idea, build on it yourself.

If you want the other person to disagree, disagree yourself.

If you want the other person to support, build on their ideas and make it clear that's what you are doing or suggest (not propose) ideas.

Q | If you want the other person to state difficulties, propose, rather than suggest, your ideas.

If you want the other person to seek clarification or information, build on their ideas or clarify yourself, because they'll want more of the same.

If you want the other person to clarify, explain and inform, ask them!

from **Face To Face Skills**, *Honey P (Gower, 1988)*

He also offers some helpful strategies for dealing with the undesirable effects of other people's behaviour:

Q | ### How to avoid being tempted into a spiral of disagreement

When someone disagrees with you, pretend to yourself that they are merely stating difficulties and not actually disagreeing. This has the advantage of making it more likely that your response is constructive.

How to cope with those who pathologically state difficulties

...pretend that their statement of difficulty is an invitation to build (or) respond by concurring with their statement and asking them for a suggestion/proposal.

How to avoid disagreeing or stating difficulties yourself

The answer is to build instead...whenever you state difficulties you are halfway to building anyway.

How to avoid losing control of the conversation

...finish whatever you have to say with a question, since we know questions are powerful shapers (of other people's behaviour).

How to get people to agree with you

...put your idea forward as a suggestion (i.e. in the form of a question) rather than a proposal (i.e. a statement, announcement or instruction). Better still, if you can build on someone else's idea, support is extremely likely. You can arrange building opportunities for yourself by seeking ideas and then disciplining yourself to build on the ones that come in response.

from **Face To Face Skills**, *Honey P, (Gower, 1988)*

Honey emphasises that this is "not a comprehensive list of behavioural antidotes" but it is certainly a useful starting point for developing your own repertoire. As you get used to the way in which your governing body operates as a group, look for opportunities to use the sort of strategies Honey describes, but adapt them to suit your personality and situation. Watch out for examples of successful strategies being used by your fellow governors and try them for yourself. You must be the best judge of what's likely to work, but it's always worth trying out a different approach, even if you're not totally sure it will work. Practice makes perfect!

The key point is that you need to find what's positive in every situation, however difficult it might be at times, and shape it, build on it, manipulate it positively for the good of the group as a whole. In time, your behaviour will influence the behaviour of others and, ultimately, the whole group.

But to ensure that you use your strategies for the good of the group as a whole you need to be clear about what the group is trying to achieve. The group's goals, your personal goals and your goals as an individual governor should be in line with each other...or should they?

Task 20
Are My Goals in Line with those of the Group?

Answer these questions

Are my goals in line with those of the group?

Should they be?

What should I do about them if they are not?

If one of my needs is to be liked and accepted, how important is that for me?

In the first two sections we looked at your personal goals and then your goals as a governor. I suggested that you revisit these from time to time in order to check that they are still your real goals and to monitor the progress you have made towards achieving them.

Goals are broad and are likely to take several years to achieve. They should represent vital aspects of your overall aim or vision. Each one should be capable of being achieved through a series of targets and associated action plans which deal with the specific, nitty-gritty details.

What are the goals of the governing body as a group, though? As we have seen, the governing body's role is essentially strategic, which implies having clear aims and objectives and a plan by which they will be achieved. These might be expressed as the aims of the school or a mission or vision statement. Many schools have developed a three to five year strategic plan within which each annual *School Development Plan* should sit comfortably. It should encompass the school's aims and objectives and interpret them in terms of one year's development.

However, we are not just talking about the *School Development Plan*, we are also talking about the governing body's development. Some governing bodies have produced their own development plans, that is, a *governing body development plan*, which becomes a part of the *School Development Plan*. These are in the minority but they represent what is possible. Where this happens, it is likely that the governing body's goals will have been made explicit. Of course, they should tie in closely with the goals for the school, but there may be some goals which are very specific to the governing body itself.

Each member of the governing body, like you, will have their own goals. They may not have thought them through as clearly as you, but they will have them, nonetheless. Those goals may be very varied and not always in the best interests of the governing body or the school as a whole. They will become apparent as time goes on and you see and hear your colleagues in action. There is little or nothing you can do about your colleagues' goals, nor should you try to do anything, other than to argue for their being made explicit, collectively, as part of the vision for the school.

What happens, though, if you and your goals seem to be in a minority? A governing body should be a democratic group, and as such, majority decisions hold sway, even if in your view the decisions are wrong. Ultimately, if you feel yourself to be too much at odds with the group as a whole, it might be better to resign and perhaps find another governing body with whose goals you are more at home. I suspect it won't come to this and it would be very sad and dramatic if it did. A very useful touchstone for governors and headteachers alike is to ask oneself: "In what way will this decision or action benefit the children?" As advocates of the child, it should be reasonably easy for the governing body to agree a set of common goals and, in my view, these need to be stated clearly and published. They then become a reference point against which to measure progress.

It's not necessarily wrong to want to be liked and accepted. It's a common human need, after all. Your colleagues are likely to have the same need, though one or two may appear to thrive on being the "odd one out". Remember "the deviant" described on page 57. It's not always the case but it is perfectly possible for the "rebel" to be right and everyone else wrong. It may be that on occasions you will be the odd one out. It's not a comfortable position and it calls upon your courage to maintain a different opinion when the majority argues against you.

It is always important in such situations to be coolly self-analytical, checking your opinion against the known facts or evidence. Ask yourself:

Have I really thought this through? If I think carefully and without prejudice about what others have argued, do they have a point or am I right? Are we both right?

You might also ask yourself:

What am I getting out of this? Do I always or frequently take on such positions? Can I live with temporary unpopularity or is it more important to me for the group to agree? (in which case I will back down.)

The answers won't be easy but you need to face up to them. You might benefit from a chat with your personal "critical friend", too.

5   Committee work

We've looked at how you might become more effective in full governing body meetings, but we've also recognised that they don't happen all that frequently. The other kind of meeting you will attend is the committee meeting. Much of what I have said about full governing body meetings applies equally to committee meetings, but there are some specific aspects of such work which merit further exposition.

Governing bodies usually set up a number of committees to help share out the work and allow people with specialised knowledge to focus on the areas they know something about. There is no legal requirement for committees. In some situations, especially where the governing body is small in number and/or is contending with medium-to long-term vacancies, it may be more appropriate to convene *ad hoc* task groups to work on particular topics, or assign responsibility to an individual rather than a group. It's always a good idea to go back to first principles when assessing the usefulness of committees and which one(s) you wish to join.

Charles Handy says:

> Committees are often better ways of "recognising" problems than "solving" problems...(they) are often, like Royal Commissions, a way of simultaneously accepting the importance of a problem but deferring its solution...
>
> The problem is this: if ...committees are convened or constructed for an inappropriate task, or with impossible constraints; if they are badly led or have ineffective procedures; if they have the wrong people, too many people, too little power or meet too infrequently; if, in short, any one part of the model is badly out of line, frustration will set in and dissonance will be created. The result will either be an activation of negative power or a badly attended non-effective group, wasting people, time and space. The chances of this happening are, in fact, very high.
>
> *from* **Understanding Organizations,** *Handy C, (Penguin Books, 1993)*

The whole point of having committees is to save time. It follows, then, that they must be clear about what they should be looking at and, especially, what decision-making powers have been delegated to them. If they can't make decisions, what's the point of setting them up in the first place? As we have seen, it's possible to set up task groups instead of committees, to investigate options and present alternatives to the governing body for decisions. If this seems to be what's required, go for it. Don't set up committees just because you think you have to.

A clear *Scheme of Delegation* should have been negotiated between the governing body and the Headteacher. This will lay out clearly who is responsible for what. It will also describe any committee structure that exists, and will probably contain the terms of reference for each committee.

Don't allow yourself to be put on a committee against your will. Too often, a new governor is expected to fill the shoes of the previous governor, without any consideration of the new colleague's skills, aptitudes, experience and expertise. You know what these are now, because you have worked through the earlier exercises, so make sure your talents are used both to your advantage and to the most effective functioning of the governing body as a whole.

In some ways, committee or task group work can be more creative and active than governing body work. You may well become involved in research and surveys; interview teachers, parents and pupils; draft proposals and recommended strategies and so on. If you have design and/or IT skills, you might become involved in various publications, such as the *Annual Report to Parents*.

Committees report back to the full governing body. Ideally, their reports would be succinct and present clear conclusions, decisions, options or actions. They should not be a fully detailed blow-by-blow commentary on how the committee came to its conclusions. Worse still is the situation where each committee Chair gives a full verbal feedback on proceedings, in addition to the written report circulated before the governing body meeting. Where this happens, it often causes a re-run of all the debates and discussions held by the committee during its meetings. In these cases, the setting up of committees and the reporting structure has actually doubled the work rather than halved or quartered it. But some governing bodies do this regularly, and it's not until someone from outside simply asks them how they operate that they realise with growing horror just what they've done.

6   Visiting the School and the Classroom

Idealy, in order to do the job properly, any governor needs to be familiar with the school in action, not just as it's reported on by the Head and others. At a basic level, the governor needs to know:

what the school looks like

what state the buildings are in

where the different classrooms are

who the teachers and support staff are and what they look like

and so on...

All schools have a "feel" to them. Some schools immediately feel oppressive or dangerous places, full of dark corridors and an air of tension. Others make the visitor feel welcome and comfortable; full of light and colour. This is not usually to do with the architecture (though this can be an obstacle at times). It's much more likely to be a reflection of the ethos of the school, its values and purpose. It's created consciously and unconsciously by everyone who works within it.

An occasional and general visit will suffice to acquaint you with the feel of the "school", though you might choose to monitor it over time.

Classroom visiting, on the other hand, is much more to do with your monitoring role in relation to the curriculum and standards of achievement in the school as a whole. Whilst it is possible to arrange this for yourself, without reference to the governing body, it makes much more sense and will be of maximum benefit to the staff and governors, if it is part of a negotiated and agreed strategy.

It's relatively easy for a governing body and teachers to agree a simple policy on governors' classroom visits. The policy should be no more than one side of A4. It should outline the purposes and benefits of the visit; the basic ground rules or protocols; a minimum commitment, expressed in terms of day or half-day equivalents and covering a year's programme of visits, to ensure a reasonable spread across the curriculum, year groups and teachers. Within such a clear framework, you can then decide the level and frequency of your personal commitment to school and classroom visiting.

This is an adapted example based on a pro-forma developed by the Governors of *The George Ward School*, Melksham, Wiltshire.

GOVERNORS' VISITS TO SCHOOL/CLASSROOM POLICY

1. Purposes/benefits

To raise governors' awareness of the life of the classroom
To develop positive relationships between teachers and governors
To help governors monitor and evaluate the work of the school, standards and pupil progress and achievement
To help the school community to know the governors

2. What it's not about

Inspection

3. Protocols

Visit planned between governor and teacher at least ten days in advance
Planning and other contextual detail provided by the teacher in advance
Focus for the visit agreed
Positive feedback to be given to the teacher and Head
Report on the visit to be included under the standing agenda item:
Governors' Classroom Visits

4. Minimum commitment

3 x 1/2 day visits per governor per year

5. Programme for the year

A programme of governors' classroom visits will be drawn up at the beginning of each academic year. The programme will ensure an even distribution of visits across subjects, year groups, classes, terms and teachers.

Governing Body, George Ward School, Melksham (1997)

Governors have, in recent years, become quite creative in finding ways of getting to grips with the curriculum and the ways in which it's taught. The following task invites you to consider the usefulness and appropriateness to your governing body of some strategies which have been used by governing bodies I know.

In Column A, tick if your governing body does or has done this. In Column B, tick if you think your governing body should do this.

Strategy	A	B
Holds Governors' meetings in school classrooms, in rotation, so that teachers can set out samples of the pupils' work (in addition to wall displays). The sample can be related to a specific agenda item and governors are invited to arrive early to spend time looking at the work.		
Includes a standing agenda item for all governing body meetings: gives feedback from governors' school/classroom visits.		
Considers the role and pros and cons of a Curriculum Committee.		
Observes a subject being taught in different year groups in order to understand progression and continuity.		
Links a governor to a class; follows it through its life in school, from year to year.		
Runs workshops for governors and parents on specific subjects.		
Reviews curriculum policies against practice: looks at gaps and contradictions.		
"Shadows" a curriculum co-ordinator.		
Sends a questionnaire to parents to establish their perceptions of the school's curriculum and achievements.		
Analyses SATs and other results data.		
Writes up Governor of the Month classroom visits in newsletter to parents.		
Reviews delegation of curriculum responsibilities.		
Becomes involved in decision-making regarding options at Key Stage 4 and the sixth form curriculum.		
Holds a social event between governors and teachers, looking at a curriculum area or theme.		
Accompanies school trips and visits.		
Obtains feedback from your local secondary school about the performance and attitude of pupils transferring from your primary school.		

Strategy cont.	A	B
Considers the potential benefits to teachers of governors' classroom visits.		
Uses feedback from Ofsted inspection as an introduction to the curriculum for new governors.		
Organises pupil presentations on aspects of the curriculum to governors.		
Attends cluster/area Heads' meetings.		
Assigns each governor to monitor a different subject/topic in the implementation of the School Development Plan.		
Arranges monitoring of the core National Curriculum subjects by Members of Curriculum Committee; and monitoring of foundation and other subject areas by the remaining governors.		
Ensures the Curriculum Committee runs workshops for parents to help explain and understand the curriculum.		
Makes presentation to teachers about the governors' roles and responsibilities.		

If, at the end of this task, you have identified a number of approaches which you think your governing body should adopt, prioritise them and think through how you can best achieve their adoption by your colleagues. Don't forget the possible strategies for shaping colleagues' responses which we explored earlier in this section. Consider possible objections to your idea as well as the support you anticipate from colleagues. Be prepared to flag your intentions clearly and build on the positives.

7   Developing Partnerships

We have looked mainly at the relationships you form with other members of your governing body, since the focus of this book is on the individual governor. However, we should acknowledge that the governing body lies at the centre of a web of vital relationships and partnerships. Margaret Hunt, Manager of Swindon Borough Council's Governor Support Unit, has identified seven key relationships:

The relationship between all governors

Governors are drawn from a wide range of backgrounds and interests and, indeed, a strength of a good governing body is that it is truly representative of the many communities it serves.

The relationship between the governing body and the headteacher

Recognised as a crucial relationship to get right. Media attention often focuses on schools where a poor relationship between the governing body and the headteacher has led to problems. Perhaps insufficient recognition is given to those governing bodies and headteachers working very effectively together.

The relationship between the governing body and the school staff

Many staff in schools remain unaware of the responsibilities of the governing body and, therefore, unclear as to why the governing body needs to gather evidence of pupils' achievements. Similarly, many governors are unsure how to go about collecting this evidence without "treading on the toes" of the professionals.

The relationship between the governing body and its committees

Whilst most governing bodies now have committee structures in place in order to spread the workload of the governing body there appear to be some governing bodies still struggling with the concept of delegation, with many committee decisions coming up for discussion again at full governing body meetings.

The relationship between the governing body, parents and the wider community

Whilst the governing body is required to account for its work through its annual report to parents and annual parents meeting, there is a widespread view that parents remain largely unaware of the role played by the governing body of a school.

The relationship between the governing body and the Local Education Authority

Most governing bodies will need to establish relationships with Local Education Authority staff across a range of service areas. It is likely that the governing body will, on occasions, want to challenge a Local Education Authority decision or proposal and on other occasions seek the support of officers with particular expertise.

The relationship between the governing body and its clerk

The work of the governing body can...be greatly assisted by the clerk to the governors, who plays an important facilitating role.

...the most productive relationships are those where the respective partners recognise and value the others' contribution. It will, perhaps, sometimes be necessary to confront the problems that prevent this mutual recognition before the relationship can become effective.

from **Relationships: Rhetoric or Reality?**, *Hunt M, (Swindon Governor, 1997)*

It is inappropriate to develop these points any further in this book and, in fact, we have looked in some detail at one or two of them in this and earlier sections. However, it is important as an individual governor to look outwards as well as inwards, bearing in mind some of John Carver's points in moving towards a new governance (see pages 43-44):

> Force an external focus and describe relationships to relevant constituencies.
>
> *from* **Boards That Make a Difference**, *Carver J, (Jossey-Bass, 1990)*

Consideration of the quality of these relationships with regard to your governing body may also provide you with a focus for an individual contribution or area for development.

8   Succession Planning and Continuity

Having now looked closely at you as a person, as a governor, and as a member of a governing body, we need to complete the picture by thinking about the future, and planning for it.

It is quite clear that you can and should develop new knowledge and skills as a governor, much of which is transferable to other areas of your life and activities, so it will not be wasted, whatever you do. During your time as a governor, you might well invest in and undertake training and development which can be used to the benefit of fellow governors and, most importantly, the children in the school.

Yet your term of office lasts for four years. I was going to write "only four years" but that would be tempting fate, since it might seem like a lot longer, if you don't have a particularly happy time. When you consider, though, just how much there is to know and do, does it not seem something of a waste to leave all that behind after a relatively short time? It can easily take up to a year before you feel confident as a new governor, which leaves three years of "productive life". The White Paper, **"Excellence In Schools"** says:

> Governors have a special role as partners in the school service; they provide a vital link between the school and the community. We shall strengthen that link by increasing the number of parent governors.
>
> *(from* **Excellence In Schools,** *DfEE (The Stationery Office Ltd., 1997, Crown Copyright)*

This comes at a time when, in some areas, it is already hard to find enough people willing to take on the role. The demand for new governors will continue to grow for the foreseeable future.

It does make sense, of course, for there to be a regular turnover of governors. It refreshes the whole governing body and ensures that elected governors are selected from the teaching staff or parents of children actually in the school at the time of the election. What, though, if you are no longer eligible to be a parent governor but feel that you still have a lot to offer and would like to continue in office at this or another school? You can put your name forward as a Local Education Authority governor or, possibly, be co-opted by colleagues. However, the **"Technical Consultation Paper: Framework for the Organisation of Schools"** accompanying the White Paper proposes:

For Community and Foundation schools, a tightening up of eligibility requirements for co-opted governors so as to restrict them to community and business interests. These might include the special community links of existing "community schools" and minor authorities.

from **Framework for the Organisation of Schools: Technical Consultation Paper**, *DfEE (The Stationery Office Ltd, 1997, Crown Copyright)*

So it may be that in the future it will be harder for some categories of experienced governors to serve more than one term of office. In many ways, this would be a waste of a very important resource.

Appointed governors can serve several terms of office. This can be a bad thing, since the appointing authority is not always best placed to know how well the governor has performed or what skills and expertise the governing body needs at the time of the appointment. It may be that continuation in office, especially by default, is counter-productive. On the positive side, however, it does provide some much needed continuity and an opportunity for the keen governor to continue to contribute valued expertise and commitment.

Continuation in office should not merely consist of "more of the same". If you stay on, you should continue to develop - by joining a different committee, for example. A good committee contains a mixture of expertise and ignorance (remember the four types of ignorance from *Section One*). If you don't feel very knowledgeable about finance, for example, and the Finance Committee contains some experienced colleagues but needs a fresh face, why not join it? Asking the simple question "Why?" can be devastatingly effective as a means of opening up a debate about the way things are done, and it's a question which the more habituated members will have stopped asking some time previously, because they feel they understand, (even if they do not!). Every committee needs someone to ask the apparently dumb question and it's much easier for the "ignorant newcomer" to do so without causing offence.

A further form of development you might consider, if you can give it the commitment it deserves, is chairing. It may be that you find yourself acting as chair or vice-chair of a committee and it is but a short step from there to becoming Chair of the governing body. As with all aspects of school governance, you need some training to do the job effectively. But first, you will want to know what it involves.

 The chairman's functions include:

- Ensuring that the business of the governing body is conducted properly, in accordance with the legal requirements.

- Ensuring that meetings are run efficiently, focusing on priorities and making best use of the time available.

- Ensuring that all members have equal opportunities to participate fully in discussions and decision making.

- Encouraging all members of the governing body to work together as a team.

- Liaising with the headteacher.

- Acting in cases which may be properly be deemed urgent.

- Making public statements on behalf of the governing body, where delegated to do so.

from **Guidance on Good Governance,** *DfEE (The Stationery Office Ltd., 1996 Crown Copyright)*

Q

It is not a job that every governor can do well and you need to be realistic about the time commitment and the range of skills and knowledge involved before accepting a suggestion that you stand for election. If you do decide to take it on, then you stand for election at the first meeting of each academic year. If you are elected - and you do the job well - you could end up doing it for a long time, since few governors have the necessary time, skills and commitment to fulfil the role of chair. On the positive side, it certainly offers a new set of challenges to the reasonably experienced governor.

If you want to know more about the role, talk to your current Chair of Governors or read the leaflet produced by the National Association of Governors and Managers on the **"Role of the Chair"**. Your Local Education Authority may well offer training specifically for Chairs of Governors.

In my experience, a good governing body will have anticipated the need for a new Chair to be waiting in the wings and will have given some thought to preparing a likely successor or two to take on the work when the current Chair stands (or sits?) down. This need not fly in the face of democracy. The governing body as a whole decides who the next Chair will be by voting for him or her. It must be in everyone's best interests to appoint somebody who is both willing and able to do the job, rather than someone who is doing it mainly because no-one else is prepared to. Maybe that successor will be you...

Whether you are prepared or able to take on such an enhanced role, you need to continue to develop as a governor, as I have said. Continue to read, attend training, learn from colleagues, help to induct new governors and improve the way the governing body works as a whole. In doing so, you will also be continuing to develop as a person - which takes us back to where we began!

Conclusion

Some Thoughts for the Future

One of the most frequent seminars run for governors in Wiltshire and Swindon is aimed at new governors. Inevitably, a vital component of the day is an explanation of the governing body's responsibilities. Up until summer 1997, I used to be able to summarise them on one side of A4 paper. It now takes two full sheets of A4. And there's more to come, what with implications for governors of the Literacy Strategy and the Numeracy Strategy to follow. Oh, and, of course, the Green Paper on Special Educational Needs.

The increase in governors' responsibilities shows no sign of relenting. At some point, it must simply become impossible for even the most effective governing body in the land to do the job. The more the responsibilities increase, the harder it will be to attract volunteers to take on the task.

And yet...

...there is a powerful argument that it's only since the Education Acts of 1986 and 1988 gave governors real responsibilities and real powers that it's become a job worth taking on. Before 1986, governorship was largely a ceremonial office. The years since then have seen a huge experiment in local democracy. Hundreds of thousands of parents, teachers, local people of all shades of opinion and all sorts of backgrounds, have taken part in that experiment. It is exciting, challenging, trail-blazing. There is nothing else like it in the world.

This book is written in that spirit of democracy, in the belief that ordinary people have a right and a responsibility to participate in the educational process. It is written in a spirit of encouragement, of offering practical solutions to the many difficulties and problems of fulfilling a hugely demanding role as a volunteer with unlimited goodwill but insufficient time to do it as well as one would like. Above all, it recognises that effective governing bodies don't happen by accident: their effectiveness depends entirely upon the individual effectiveness of the human beings who take on the role. I hope that I have played some small part in ensuring that those human beings find fulfilment in the work and help to make all our schools improve continuously.

Appendix I

The Roles of Governing Bodies

Steering

- agreeing the aims and values of the school
- setting a policy on the curriculum, including any requirement for special educational needs
- setting budgets and approving school development plans
- responding to inspection reports and publishing a post-inspection action plan

Monitoring

- making sure that the school adheres to its policies, budgets and plans
- keeping informed about the quality and standards of education in the school, including pupil achievement

Executive

- taking direct responsibility for recruitment of senior staff and some disciplinary matters, while recognising the headteacher's responsibility for managing the school
- contributing to the admissions policy and appeals system

Accountability

- making sure that parents are kept informed about what is happening in the school through the annual report and annual meeting for parents
- taking parents' views into account

Support

- supporting and advising headteachers
- providing practical help and skill

from **Lessons In Teamwork: How School Governing Bodies Can Become More Effective**, *Audit Commission/Ofsted (The Stationery Office Ltd., 1995 Crown Copyright)*

The Responsibilities of Governing Bodies

Curriculum

- ensure that it is broad and balanced
- ensure that the National Curriculum and its assessment procedures are carried out in full (with the Head)
- decide whether the school should provide sex education and keep a written record (Primary schools)
- have a sex education policy, including content and organisation (Secondary)
- develop and publish a policy for religious education and collective worship
- hear formal complaints about the curriculum
- adapt the LEA's curriculum policy to match school aims
- send assessment results to appropriate bodies
- ensure political balance in presentation of curriculum
- hear appeals against Head's decision to lift or change National Curriculum requirements for a child

Finance

- agree the school's spending plan
- monitor the spending, receiving statements from the LEA which must be available for inspection
- must be consulted on any changes to the LMS scheme
- must draw up a charging policy
- may charge for optional extra-curricular activities
- may not charge for any curricular activities except instrumental tuition
- may invite voluntary contributions towards any aspect of the school's work

Personnel

- decide on staffing levels
- agree all staffing procedures, including disciplinary rules, keeping to relevant parts of employment law
- appoint, suspend and dismiss staff
- make a range of decisions on pay for teaching staff
- review the pay of Head and Deputy(ies) annually
- hear staff grievances
- ensure that the school keeps to the LEA's appraisal arrangements

Admissions

- be consulted on LEA's admissions arrangements annually
- may prepare a statement on their admissions policy
- must publish the admissions arrangements in the school prospectus
- can ask the LEA to raise the admissions limit and appeal to Secretary of State if dissatisfied
- must meet the parents' choice of school (some exceptions)

Conduct

- determine general principles of discipline policy
- may direct the Head to reinstate excluded pupils
- must keep an admissions and (authorised and unauthorised) attendance register, reporting to the LEA
- must include information on absences in the prospectus and annual report, sending the information to be included in performance tables
- decide when the school day begins and ends
- can make pupils attend lessons outside school premises, other than for RE

Providing information

- must give the LEA and Secretary of State any information requested
- must publish a school prospectus and an annual report for parents
- must maintain pupils' educational records
- must give Year 11 pupils information from local FE colleges
- must run an annual parents' meeting

School inspections

- can comment on the plan for the inspection
- must tell parents and others about the inspection
- must arrange a meeting between the Registered Inspector (RI) and parents
- must give relevant information to the RI
- must send out the inspection report and its summary
- must draw up an action plan and publish it to parents and others
- must report on progress on the implementation of the plan in the annual report

Premises

- ensure health and safety
- ensure maintenance of all school plant
- control the use of the premises outside the school day, including use by the community
- may keep any income thus derived
- must follow any reasonable directions from the LEA

from **School Governors: A Guide to the Law,** *DfEE (The Stationery Office Ltd., 1997 Crown Copyright)*

Bibliography

Anon.	**School Governors: A Guide to the Law** (DfEE, 1997)
Anon.	**Excellence in Schools** (The Stationery Office, 1997)
Anon.	**Framework for the Organisation of Schools** (DfEE, 1997)
Anon.	**Guidance on Good Governance** (DfEE, 1996)
Anon.	**Teamwork for School Improvement** (DfEE, 1996)
Audit Commission /Ofsted,	**Lesson in Teamwork** (HMSO, 1995)
Barber, M et al	**Governing Bodies and Effective Schools** (DfEE, 1995)
Belbin, R M	**Management Teams - Why They Succeed or Fail** (Butterworth-Heinemann, 1981)
Bettleheim, B	**A Good Enough Parent** (Vantage Books, 1987)
Carver, John	**Boards That Make A Difference** (Jossey-Bass, 1990)
Handy, Charles	**Understanding Organizations** (Penguin, 1993)
Honey, Peter	**Face to Face Skills** (Gower, 1988)
Hunt, J	**Managing People at Work** (McGraw-Hill, 1992)
Hunt, Margaret	**Relationships: Rhetoric or Reality?** (Swindon Borough Council, 1997)
Nolan Committee	**Second Report of the Committee on Standards in Public Life** (The Stationery Office, 1995)
Ofsted	**The Inspection Resource Pack** (The Stationery Office, 1995)
Wiltshire County Council	**Governing Schools Effectively Right From The Start** (CD ROM Wiltshire CC, County Hall, Bythesea Road, Trowbridge, Wiltshire, 1997)
Woodhead, Chris	**Annual Report of HMCI** (The Stationery Office, 1996)

Resources and Further Reading

Anon.	**Effective Governors' Meetings** (NAGM, 1996)
Anon.	**Manual for Clerks and Governing Bodies** (ISCG, 1995)
Anon.	**Meeting To Decide** (BBC Video, 1990)
Anon.	**The Effective Governing Body**, (NAGM, 1996)
Anon.	**The Role of the Chair** (NAGM, 1994)
Anon.	**Using Your Time Well** (AGIT, 1996)
Creese, Michael	**Effective Governors, Effective Schools** (Fulton, 1995)
Earley, Peter	**School Governing Bodies: Making Progress?** (NFER, 1994)
Esp, D and Sarah,	**Effective Governors for Effective Schools** (Pitman, 1995)
Pounce, Martin	**The Effective Committee Series** (Calibre Learning, 1996)
Russell, Sheila	**Collaborative School Self-Review** (Lemos/Crane, 1996)
Sallis, Joan	**Basics for School Governors** (Network Educational Press, 1993)
Sallis, Joan	**Heads and Governors: Building the Partnership** (AGIT, 1994)
Thody, Angela	**School Governors: Leaders or Followers?** (Longman, 1994)
Wolfendale, Sheila	**Empowering Parents and Teachers** (Cassell, 1993)

"The Effective School Governor" is the tenth title in *The School Effectiveness Series,* which focuses on practical and useful ideas for individual schools and teachers. This series addresses the issues of whole school improvement along with new knowledge about teaching and learning, and offers straightforward solutions which teachers can use to make life more rewarding for themselves and those they teach.

Book 1: *Accelerated Learning in the Classroom* by Alistair Smith
ISBN: 1-85539-034-5   £15.95

- The first book in the UK to apply new knowledge about the brain to classroom practice
- Contains practical methods so teachers can apply accelerated learning theories to their own classrooms
- Aims to increase the pace of learning and deepen understanding
- Includes advice on how to create the ideal enviroment for learning and how to help learners fulfil their potential
- Offers practical solutions on improving performance, motivation and understanding

Book 2: *Effective Learning Activities* by Chris Dickinson
ISBN: 1-85539-035-3   £8.95

- An essential teaching guide which focuses on practical activities to improve learning
- Aims to improve results through effective learning, which will raise achievement, deepen understanding, promote self-esteem and improve motivation
- Includes activities which are designed to promote differentiation and understanding
- Includes activities suitable for GCSE, National Curriculum, Highers, GSVQ and GNVQ

Book 3: *Effective Heads of Department* by Phil Jones & Nick Sparks
ISBN: 1-85539-036-1   £8.95

- Contains a range of practical systems and approaches; each of the eight sections ends with a 'checklist for action'
- Designed to develop practice in line with OFSTED expectations and DfEE thinking by monitoring and improving quality
- Addresses issues such as managing resources, leadership, learning, departmental planning and making assessment valuable
- Includes useful information for senior managers in schools who are looking to enhance the effectiveness of their Heads of Department

Book 4: *Lessons are for Learning* by Mike Hughes
ISBN: 1-85539-038-8   £11.95

- Brings together the theory of learning with the realities of the classroom environment
- Encourages teachers to reflect on their own classroom practice and challenges them to think about why they teach in the way they do
- Offers practical suggestions for activities that bridge the gap between recent developments in the theory of learning and the constraints in classroom teaching
- Ideal for stimulating thought and generating discussion

Book 5: *Effective Learning in Science* by Paul Denley and Keith Bishop
ISBN: 1-85539-039-6   £11.95

- Encourages discussion about the aims and purposes in teaching science and the role of subject knowledge in effective teaching
- Tackles issues such as planning for effective learning, the use of resources and other relevant management issues
- Offers help in the development of a departmental plan to revise schemes of work, resources, classroom strategies, in order to make learning and teaching more effective
- Ideal for any science department aiming to increase performance and improve results

Book 6: *Raising Boys' Achievement* by Jon Pickering
ISBN: 1-85539-040-X £11.95

- Addresses the causes of boys' underachievement and offers possible solutions
- Focuses the search for causes and solutions on teachers working in the classroom
- Looks at examples of good practice in schools to help guide the planning and implementation of strategies to raise achievement
- Offers practical, 'real' solutions, along with tried and tested training suggestions
- Ideal as a basis for INSET or as a guide to practical activities for classroom teachers

Book 7: *Effective Provision for Able & Talented Children* by Barry Teare
ISBN: 1-85539-041-8 £11.95

- Basic theory, necessary procedures and turning theory into practice
- Main methods of identifying the able and talented
- Concerns about achievement and appropriate strategies to raise achievement
- The role of the classroom teacher, monitoring and evaluation techniques
- Practical enrichment activities and appropriate resources

Book 8: *Effective Careers Education & Guidance* by Andrew Edwards and Anthony Barnes
ISBN: 1-85539-045-0 £11.95

- Strategic planning of the careers programme as part of the wider curriculum
- Practical consideration of managing careers education and guidance
- Practical activities for reflection and personal learning, and case studies where such activities have been used
- Aspects of guidance and counselling involved in helping students to understand their own capabilities and form career plans
- Strategies for reviewing and developing existing practice

Book 9: *Best behaviour and Best behaviour FIRST AID* by Peter Relf, Rod Hirst,
Jan Richardson and GeorginaYoudell

ISBN: 1-85539-046-9 £12.95

- Provides support for those who seek starting points for effective behaviour management, for individual teachers and for middle and senior managers
- Focuses on practical and useful ideas for individual schools and teachers

Best behaviour FIRST AID
ISBN: 1-85539-047-7 £10.50 (pack of 5 booklets)

- Provides strategies to cope with aggression, defiance and disturbance
- Straightforward action points for self-esteem

Other Publications

Accelerated Learning in Practice by Alistair Smith
ISBN: 1-85539-048-5 £19.95

- The author's second book which takes Nobel Prize winning brain research into the classroom.
- Structured to help readers access and retain the information necessary to begin to accelerate their own learning and that of the students they teach.
- Contains over 100 learning tools, case studies from 36 schools and an up to the minute resources section.
- Includes 9 principles of learning based on brain research and the author's 7 Stage Accelerated Learning cycle.

Primary Publications

Imagine That... by Stephen Bowkett
ISBN: 1-85539-043-4   £19.95

- Hands-on, user-friendly manual for stimulating creative thinking, talking and writing in the classroom
- Provides over 100 practical and immediately useable classroom activities and games that can be used in isolation, or in combination, to help meet the requirements and standards of the National Curriculum
- Explores the nature of creative thinking and how this can be effectively driven through an ethos of positive encouragement, mutual support and celebration of success and achievement
- Empowers children to learn how to learn

Helping With Reading by Anne Butterworth and Angela White
ISBN: 1-85539-044-2   £14.95

- Includes sections on 'Hearing Children Read', 'Word Recognition' and 'Phonics'
- Provides precisely focused, easily implemented follow-up activities for pupils who need extra reinforcement of basic reading skills
- Activities which directly relate to the National Curriculum and 'Literacy Hour' group work. They are clear, practical and easily implemented. Ideas and activities can also be incorporated into Individual Education Plans
- Aims to address current concerns about reading standards and to provide support in view of the growing use of classroom assistants and parents to help with the teaching of reading